ROYAL COURT THEATRE PRODUCTIONS

in association with
Ambassador Theatre Group and Criterion Productions plc present

The Weir

by Conor McPherson

First performed at the Royal Court Theatre Upstairs
West Street, London on 4th July 1997

First performance at the Duke of York's Theatre
St Martin's Lane, London on 8th October 1998

The Weir

by Conor McPherson

Cast in order of appearance
Jack **Karl Johnson**
Brendan **Daniel Flynn**
Jim **Anthony O'Donnell**
Finbar **Miles Anderson**
Valerie **Ruth Gemmell**

Director **Ian Rickson**
Designer **Rae Smith**
Lighting Designer **Paule Constable**
Sound Designer **Paul Arditti**
Assistant Director **Yvonne McDevitt**
Production Manager **Edwyn Wilson**
Company Stage Manager **Cath Binks**
Stage Manager **Sara Crosdale**
Deputy Stage Manager **Marion Spon**
Costume Supervisor **Iona Kenrick**
Dialect Coach **Joan Washington**
Voice Coach **Patsy Rodenburg**
Set Construction **Stage Surgeons Ltd & Scott Fleary Schofield**
Painted by **Paddy Hamilton**
Production Photography **Joe Dilworth**

Royal Court Theatre Productions would like to thank the following for their help with this production: For background research: Mary Boley, Professor Emeritus Arthur J. Ellison, June Kosoff of Cruse Bereavement Care, Alan Moorehouse, Julia Reid, Dr Mike Shooter. Legal Advice: Harrison Curtis Solicitors. Auditorium ceiling constructed by Stage Surgeons Ltd (020-7237 2765), rigged and suspended by Vertigo Rigging Ltd; Wardrobe care by Persil and Comfort courtesy of Lever Brothers Ltd, refrigerators by Electrolux and Philips Major Appliances Ltd.; kettles by Morphy Richards; video for casting purposes by Hitachi; backstage coffee machine by West 9; furniture by Knoll International; freezer for backstage use supplied by Zanussi Ltd 'Now that's a good idea.' Closed circuit TV cameras and monitors by Mitsubishi UK Ltd. Natural spring water from Aqua Cool, 12 Waterside Way, London SW17 0XH, tel. 020-8947 5666. Overhead projector from W.H. Smith; Sanyo U.K for the backstage microwave. Thanks to Habitat. Cat care by Petsmart, Hill's Pet Nutrition and Spillers Petfoods. Herbal cigarettes kindly donated by Honeyrose Products Ltd, Stowmarket.
Page one photography by Joanne O'Brien; page two by Ivan Kyncl.

THE COMPANY

Conor McPherson (writer)
For the Royal Court: The Weir, Dublin Carol.
Theatre includes: This Lime Tree Bower, St
Nicholas (Bush); The Good Thief, Rum and
Vodka (Fly By Night Theatre Company, Dublin).
Radio: This Lime Tree Bower, The Weir.
Film: I Went Down.

Miles Anderson
Theatre includes: Henry IV Parts I & II, Twelfth
Night, Macbeth, Peter Pan, The Witch of
Edmonton, The Twin Rivals, Money, Life's a
Dream (RSC); When We Dead Awaken
(Almeida); The Bullet (Donmar); The Rehearsal
(Garrick); Oliver (Palladium).
Television includes: Robin Hood, The Sweeney,
Lorna Doone, House of Cards, Soldier Soldier,
The Rector's Wife, Oliver's Travels, A Touch of
Frost, Midsomer Murders, Doomwatch, Have
Your Cake and Eat It, Every Woman Knows A
Secret.
Films includes: Fast Food, Joseph Andrews, The
39 Steps, Gunbus, Cry Freedom, A Far Off
Place, Riddler's Moon, The King is Alive,
Dogmes.

Paul Arditti (sound designer)
Paul Arditti has been designing sound for theatre
since 1983. He currently combines his post as
Head of Sound at the Royal Court (where he has
designed more than 40 productions) with regular
freelance projects.
For the Royal Court: Dublin Carol, The Kitchen,
Rat in the Skull, Some Voices, Mojo, The Lights,
The Weir, The Steward of Christendom,
Shopping and Fucking, Blue Heart, (co-produc-
tions with Out of Joint). The Chairs (co-produc-
tion with Theatre de Complicite); The Strip,
Never Land, Cleansed, Via Dolorosa, Real Classy
Affair and the 1998 Young Writers' Festival
'Choice'.
Other theatre includes: Our Lady of Sligo (RNT
with Out of Joint); Some Explicit Polaroids (Out
of Joint); Hamlet, The Tempest (RSC); Orpheus
Descending, Cyrano de Bergerac, St Joan (West
End); Marathon (Gate).
Musicals include: Doctor Dolittle, Piaf, The
Threepenny Opera.
Awards include: Drama Desk Award for
Outstanding Sound Design 1992 for Four
Baboons Adoring the Sun (Broadway).

Paule Constable (lighting designer)
For the Royal Court: Dublin Carol, The Weir,
The Glory of Living.
Other theatre includes: Tales from Ovid, The
Dispute, Uncle Vanya, Beckett 'Shorts', The
Mysteries (RSC); The Darker Face of the Earth,
Haroun and the Sea of Stories, Caucasian Chalk
Circle (RNT); Amadeus (West End, Broadway,
Olivier nomination); Les Misérables (Tel Aviv);
Playhouse Creatures (Old Vic); More Grimms'
Tales (Young Vic and New York); four
productions for Theatre de Complicité
including the Olivier-nominated Street of
Crocodiles.
Opera includes: ENO, Welsh National Opera,
Scottish Opera, Opera North, New Zealand
International Festival.

Daniel Flynn
At the Royal Court: I Am Yours (for Shared
Experience).
Other theatre includes: An Act of Faith, The
Madness of George III (RNT); Hamlet (RNT
Tour); A Chorus of Disapproval (Scarborough &
RNT); Anna Christie, The Winter's Tale (Young
Vic); The Glass Menagerie (Young Vic tour);
Translations (Donmar Warehouse); Macbeth
(Riverside Studios); A Midsummer Night's
Dream, Troilus & Cressida (Regents Park Open
Air Theatre); The Tempest, Bingo (RSC Tour);
Woman In Mind (Vaudeville); Twelfth Night
(Sheffield); Chips With Everything (Leeds
Playhouse).
Television includes: The Peter Principle, Peak
Practice, Bugs, The Choir, Soldier Soldier, A
Breed of Heroes, The Detectives, Casualty, The
Buddha of Suburbia, The Bill, No Excuses, The
Two Gentlemen of Verona, Goodbye Mr Chips,
Kit Curran, Call Me Mister, The Two of Us,
Heidi.
Film includes: Biggles.

Ruth Gemmell
Theatre includes: Uncle Vanya, An Ideal
Husband, The Importance of Being Earnest
(Lyceum, Edinburgh); The Winter's Tale, The
Second Mrs Tanqueray (Salisbury Playhouse);
Nabokov's Gloves (Hampstead), A Tale of Two
Cities (Citizens, Glasgow), Tis A Pity She's A
Whore, The Country Wife (Lancaster
Playhouse), Measure For Measure (Chester),
The Turn of the Screw (Hornchurch), Othello
(Railway Tavern).
Television includes: The Perfect Blue, The
Alchemists, Silent Witness, Band of Gold, The
Bill, Four Fathers, Macbeth, Peak Practice,
Kavanagh Q.C., In Suspicious Circumstances,
You Me & It, Who Needs A Heart, Miller
Shorts.
Film includes: Fever Pitch.
Short films include: Everywhere, A Stiff Drink,
Mea Culpa.
Radio includes: Maestro, Fireworks, The
Candlemass Road, Woman of Juda, Teen Love,
The House (BBC Radio 4).

Karl Johnson
For the Royal Court: Been So Long, Just a Little
Less than Normal, Sudlow's Dawn, Irish Eyes
and English Tears.
Other theatre includes: Cardiff East, The Ends of
the Earth, The Machine Wreckers, Black Snow,
The Resistible Rise of Arturo Ui, The Sea, Uncle
Vanya, A Midsummer Night's Dream, Glengarry
Glen Ross, Wild Honey, The Mysteries, Tim
Page's Nam (RNT); In the Company of Men, TV
Times, Knight of the Burning Pestle (RSC);
Amadeus (Peter Hall Company); Woyzeck (Lyric,
Hammersmith); War Crimes (ICA); The Dresser
(Thorndike, Leatherhead); Hedda Gabler
(Yvonne Arnauld, Guildford); As You Like It (Old
Vic), Vieux Carre (Piccadilly).
Television includes: David Copperfield, Vanity
Fair, The Temptation of Franz Schubert, Wing
and a Prayer, An Independent Man, As You Like
It, Catherine The Great, Lifeboat, Glassing
Gareth, Judas and The Gimp, Sexual Intercourse
Began in 1963, The Shawl, A Tale of Two Cities,
Rules of Engagement, Poirot, Casualty, The Bill,
Boon, Bergerac, Sons and Lovers, Rock Follies of
77, Chips With Everything.
Films include: Love is the Devil, Wittgenstein,
Close My Eyes, Prick Up Your Ears, Jubilee, The
Tempest, The Tent, The Magic Shop.

Yvonne McDevitt (assistant director)
For the Royal Court as Assistant: Dublin Carol.
Other theatre as Assistant: The Meeting, Kill the
Old, Torture the Young, Perfect Days (Traverse);
The Invisible Woman (Gate); Madame Butterfly
(Robert Wilson, L'Opera Bastille).
Other theatre as Director: Acts (Traverse); The
Lottery Ticket (The Red Room); Not I, Rockaby
(Dublin Fringe Festival / Hermitage, Moscow).

Anthony O'Donnell
For the Royal Court: Cloud Nine.
Other theatre includes: Uncle Vanya
(Hampstead); A Midsummer Night's Dream,
Our Friends in The North, Peter Pan, A New
Way to Pay Old Debts, Measure for Measure,
All's Well That Ends Well, Comedy of Errors,
Beggars Opera, As You Like It, Life's a Dream
(RSC); Bartholomew Fair, Ghetto, The Miser,
The Resistible Rise of Arturo Ui, Under Milk
Wood, The Way of The World, The London
Cuckolds (RNT); Glengarry Glen Ross, Galileo,
Dance of Death, Ivanov (Almeida).
Television includes: A Very Peculiar Practice,
Minder, Merchant of Venice, Moll Flanders, Pie in
The Sky, Tess, Leprechauns, Nuts in May
Films include: Santa Claus, Car Trouble, Hawks,
Robin Hood, Secrets and Lies, The Barber of
Siberia, O Xango De Baker Street (Brasil),
Love's Labours Lost.

Ian Rickson (director)
Ian Rickson is the Artistic Director of the Royal
Court.
For the Royal Court: Dublin Carol, The Weir
(Theatre Upstairs and Theatre Downstairs),
The Lights, Pale Horse, Mojo (& Steppenwolf
Theatre Co., Chicago), Ashes and Sand, Some
Voices, Killers (1992 Young Writers' Festival),
Wildfire.
Other theatre includes: The Day I Stood Still
(RNT); The House of Yes (Gate Theatre,
London); Me and My Friend (Chichester
Festival Theatre); Queer Fish (BAC); First
Strike (Soho Poly).
Opera includes: La Serva Padrona (Broomhill).

Rae Smith (designer)
For the Royal Court: Dublin Carol, The Weir,
Some Voices, Trust.
Other theatre includes: Cause Celebre,
Sarasine, Mrs Warren's Profession, A Christmas
Carol, The Letter (Lyric Hammersmith); The
Cocktail Party, A Midsummer Night's Dream
(Lyceum, Edinburgh); Endgame, Juno and the
Paycock (Donmar Warehouse); Silence, Silence,
Silence (Mladinsko Theatre, Slovenia); The
Phoenician Women, Henry IV (RSC); The Visit,
Help I'm Alive, Ave Maria, The Street of
Crocodiles (Theatre de Complicite).
Opera includes: Don Giovanni (Welsh National
Opera); The Magic Flute (Opera North);
Shameless (Opera Circus); The Maids (Lyric
Hammersmith).
Rae has also directed and designed Lucky
(David Glass Ensemble); Mysteria (RSC) and is
currently working on The Terminatrix (National
Theatre Studio / ENO). She has received two
design awards for working sabbaticals in
Indonesia and Japan. Future productions
include: La Finta Semplice (Royal Opera House
Studio); The Way of The World (Royal
Exchange, Manchester).
www.rae-smith.co.uk

THE ENGLISH STAGE COMPANY AT THE ROYAL COURT

The English Stage Company at the Royal Court opened in 1956 as a subsidised theatre producing new British plays, international plays and some classical revivals.

The first artistic director George Devine aimed to create a writers' theatre, 'a place where the dramatist is acknowledged as the fundamental creative force in the theatre and where the play is more important than the actors, the director, the designer'. The urgent need was to find a contemporary style in which the play, the acting, direction and design are all combined. He believed that 'the battle will be a long one to continue to create the right conditions for writers to work in'.

Devine aimed to discover 'hard-hitting, uncompromising writers whose plays are stimulating, provocative and exciting'. The Royal Court production of John Osborne's Look Back in Anger in May 1956 is now seen as the decisive starting point of modern British drama, and the policy created a new generation of British playwrights. The first wave included John Osborne, Arnold Wesker, John Arden, Ann Jellicoe, N F Simpson and Edward Bond. Early seasons included new international plays by Bertolt Brecht, Eugène Ionesco, Samuel Beckett, Jean-Paul Sartre and Marguerite Duras.

The theatre started with the 400-seat proscenium arch Theatre Downstairs, and then in 1969 opened a second theatre, the 60-seat studio Theatre Upstairs. Productions in the Theatre Upstairs have transferred to the West End, such as Conor McPherson's The Weir, Kevin Elyot's My Night With Reg and Ariel Dorfman's Death and the Maiden. The Royal Court also co-produces plays which have transferred to the West End or toured internationally, such as Sebastian Barry's The Steward of Christendom and Mark Ravenhill's Shopping and Fucking (with Out of Joint), Martin McDonagh's The Beauty Queen Of Leenane (with Druid Theatre Company), Ayub Khan-Din's East is East (with Tamasha Theatre Company, and now a feature film).

Since 1994 the Royal Court's artistic policy has again been vigorously directed to finding a new generation of playwrights. The writers include Joe Penhall, Rebecca Prichard, Michael Wynne, Nick Grosso, Judy Upton, Meredith Oakes, Sarah Kane, Anthony Neilson, Judith Johnson, James Stock, Jez Butterworth, Simon Block, Martin McDonagh, Mark Ravenhill, Ayub Khan-Din, Tamantha Hammerschlag, Jess Walters, Conor McPherson, Simon Stephens, Richard

Bean, Roy Williams, Gary Mitchell, Mick Mahoney, Rebecca Gilman, Christopher Shinn and Kia Corthron. This expanded programme of new plays has been made possible through the support of the Jerwood Foundation, and many in association with the Royal National Theatre Studio.

In recent years there have been record-breaking productions at the box office, with capacity houses for Jez Butterworth's Mojo, Sebastian Barry's The Steward of Christendom, Martin McDonagh's The Beauty Queen of Leenane, Ayub Khan-Din's East is East, Eugène Ionesco's The Chairs and Conor McPherson's The Weir, which transferred to the West End in October 1998, is now running at the Duke of York's Theatre.

The newly refurbished theatre in Sloane Square opened in February 2000, with a policy still inspired by the first artistic director George Devine. The Royal Court is an international theatre for new plays and new playwrights, and the work shapes contemporary drama in Britain and overseas.

AWARDS FOR
THE ROYAL COURT

Ariel Dorfman's Death and the Maiden and John Guare's Six Degrees of Separation won the Olivier Award for Best Play in 1992 and 1993 respectively. Terry Johnson's Hysteria won the 1994 Olivier Award for Best Comedy, and also the Writers' Guild Award for Best West End Play. Kevin Elyot's My Night with Reg won the 1994 Writers' Guild Award for Best Fringe Play, the Evening Standard Award for Best Comedy, and the 1994 Olivier Award for Best Comedy. Joe Penhall was joint winner of the 1994 John Whiting Award for Some Voices. Sebastian Barry won the 1995 Writers' Guild Award for Best Fringe Play, the 1995 Critics' Circle Award and the 1997 Christopher Ewart-Biggs Literary Prize for The Steward of Christendom, and the 1995 Lloyds Private Banking Playwright of the Year Award. Jez Butterworth won the 1995 George Devine Award for Most Promising Playwright, the 1995 Writers' Guild New Writer of the Year Award, the Evening Standard Award for Most Promising Playwright and the 1995 Olivier Award for Best Comedy for Mojo. Phyllis Nagy won the 1995 Writers' Guild Award for Best Regional Play for Disappeared.

Michael Wynne won the 1996 Meyer-Whitworth Award for The Knocky. Martin McDonagh won the 1996 George Devine Award, the 1996 Writers' Guild Best Fringe Play Award, the 1996 Critics' Circle Award and the 1996 Evening Standard Award for Most Promising Playwright for The Beauty Queen of Leenane. Marina Carr won the 19th Susan Smith Blackburn Prize (1996/7) for Portia Coughlan. Conor McPherson won the 1997 George Devine Award, the 1997 Critics' Circle Award and the 1997 Evening Standard Award for Most Promising Playwright for The Weir. Ayub Khan-Din won the 1997 Writers' Guild Award for Best West End Play, the 1997 Writers' Guild New Writer of the Year Award and the 1996 John Whiting Award for East is East. Anthony Neilson won the 1997 Writers' Guild Award for Best Fringe Play for The Censor. The Royal Court was the overall winner of the 1995 Prudential Award for the Arts for creativity, excellence, innovation and accessibility. The Royal Court Theatre Upstairs won the 1995 Peter Brook Empty Space Award for innovation and excellence in theatre.

At the 1998 Tony Awards, Martin McDonagh's The Beauty Queen of Leenane (co-production with Druid Theatre Company) won four awards including Garry Hynes for Best Director and was nominated for a further two. Eugene Ionesco's The Chairs (co-production with Theatre de Complicite) was nominated for six Tony awards. David Hare won the 1998 Time Out Live Award for Outstanding Achievement for Via Dolorosa. Sarah Kane won the 1998 Arts Foundation Fellowship in Playwriting. Rebecca Prichard won the 1998 Critics' Circle Award for Most Promising Playwright for Yard Gal.

Conor McPherson won the 1999 Olivier Award for Best New Play for The Weir. The Royal Court won the 1999 ITI Award for Excellence in International Theatre. Sarah Kane's Cleansed was awarded Best Foreign Language Play in 1999 by Theater Heute in Germany. Rebecca Gilman won the 1999 Evening Standard Award for Most Promising Playwright for The Glory of Living.

In 1999, the Royal Court won the European theatre prize New Theatrical Realities, presented at Taormina Arte in Sicily, for its efforts in recent years in discovering and producing the work of young British dramatists.

RE-BUILDING THE ROYAL COURT

In 1995, the Royal Court was awarded a National Lottery grant through the Arts Council of England, to pay for three quarters of a £26m project to re-build completely our 100-year old home. The rules of the award required the Royal Court to raise £7.5m in partnership funding. The building has been completed thanks to the generous support of those listed below. We are particularly grateful for the contributions of over 5,500 audience members.

If you would like to support the ongoing work of the Royal Court please contact the Development Department on 020 7565 5050.

PROGRAMME SUPPORTERS

The Royal Court (English Stage Company Ltd) receives its principal funding from the Arts Council of England. It is also supported financially by a wide range of private companies and public bodies and earns the remainder of its income from the box office and its own trading activities. The Royal Borough of Kensington & Chelsea gives an annual grant to the Royal Court Young Writers' Programme and the London Boroughs Grants Committee provides project funding for a number of play development initiatives.

This year the Jerwood Charitable Foundation continues to support new plays by new playwrights with the fifth series of Jerwood New Playwrights. Since 1993 the A.S.K. Theater Projects of Los Angeles has funded a Playwrights' Programme at the theatre. Bloomberg Mondays, a continuation of the Royal Court's reduced price ticket scheme, is supported by Bloomberg News. BSkyB have also generously committed to a two-year sponsorship of the Royal Court Young Writers' Festival.

Royal Court Registered Charity number 231242.

TRUSTS AND FOUNDATIONS
American Friends of the Royal Court Theatre
Jerwood Charitable Foundation
Laura Pels Foundation
The Peggy Ramsay Foundation
The John Lyons Charity
The Alan & Babette Sainsbury Charitable Fund
The John Studzinski Foundation
The Bulldog Princep Theatrical Fund
The Trusthouse Charitable Foundation

MAJOR SPONSORS
Marks and Spencer
Barclays Bank plc
Bloomberg News
BSkyB
Francis Finlay
Virgin Atlantic

BUSINESS MEMBERS
Agnès B
Cartier
Channel Four Television
Davis Polk & Wardwell
Goldman Sachs International
Laporte plc
Lazard Brothers & Co. Ltd
Lee and Pembertons
Mask
Mishcon de Reya Solicitors
Redwood Publishing plc
Simons Muirhead & Burton
Space NK
J Walter Thompson

INDIVIDUAL MEMBERS
Patrons
Advanpress
Associated Newspapers Ltd
Mrs Alan Campbell-Johnson
Gill Carrick
Citigate Dewe Rogerson Ltd
Conway van Gelder
Chris Corbin
David Day
Greg Dyke
Ralph A Fields
Mike Frain
Judy & Frank Grace
Homevale Ltd
JHJ and SF Lewis
Lex Service plc
Barbara Minto
New Penny Productions Ltd
Martin Newson
AT Poeton & Son Ltd.
Greville Poke
David Rowland
Sir George Russell
Mr & Mrs Anthony Weden
Richard Wilson
George & Moira Yip

Benefactors
Bill Andrewes
Batia Asher
Elaine Mitchell Attias
Jeremy Bond
Katie Bradford
Julian Brookstone
Yuen-Wei Chew
Carole & Neville Conrad
Coppard and Co.
Curtis Brown Ltd
Robyn Durie
Winston Fletcher
Claire & William Frankel
Nicholas A Fraser
Robert Freeman
Norman Gerard
Henny Gestetner OBE
Carolyn Goldbart
Sally Greene
Angela Heylin
Juliet Horsman
Amanda Howard Associates
ICM Ltd
Trevor Ingman
IPA
Lisa C Irwin
Peter Jones
Paul Kaju & Jane Peterson
Catherine Be Kemeny
Thomas & Nancy Kemeny
KPMG
CA Leng
Lady Lever
Colette & Peter Levy
Mae Modiano
Pat Morton
Joan Moynihan
Paul Oppenheimer
Mr & Mrs Michael Orr
Sir Eric Parker
Carol Rayman
Angharad Rees
John & Rosemarie Reynolds
John Ritchie
John Sandoe (Books) Ltd
Nicholas Selmes
Peregrine Simon
David & Patricia Smalley
Max Stafford-Clark
Sue Stapely
Ann Marie Starr
Charlotte Watcyn Lewis

AMERICAN FRIENDS
Founders
Victoria & David Elenowitz
Francis Finlay
Monica Gerard-Sharp & Ali Wambold
Donald & Mia Martin Glickman
Carl Icahn & Gail Golden
Jeanne Hauswald
Mary Ellen Johnson & Richard Goeltz
Dany Khosrovani
Kay Koplointz
Stephen Magowan
Monica Menell-Kinberg PhD
Benjamin Rauch & Margaret Scott
Rory Riggs
Robert Rosenkranz
Gerald Schoenfeld

Patrons
Miriam Bienstock
Arthur Bellinzoni
Robert L & Janice Billingsley
Harry Brown
Catherine G Curran
Leni Darrow
Michael & Linda Donovan
April Foley
Richard & Linda Gelfond
The Howard Gilman Foundation
Richard & Marcia Grand
Paul Hallingby
Herrick Theatre Foundation
Maurice & Jean R Jacobs
Sahra T Lese
Susan & Martin Lipton
Anne Locksley
William & Hilary Russell
Howard & Barbara Sloan
Margaret Jackson Smith
Mika Sterling
Arielle Tepper
The Thorne Foundation

Benefactors
Tom Armstrong
Mr & Mrs Mark Arnold
Elaine Attias
Denise & Matthew Chapman
Richard & Rosalind Edelman
Abe & Florence Elenowitz
Hiram & Barbara Gordon
Brian & Araceli Keelan
Jennifer CE Laing
Burt Lerner
Rudolph Rauch
Lawrence & Helen Remmel
Robert & Nancy Scully
Julie Talen

THE WEIR AT THE DUKE OF YORKS

Executive Director
Vikki Heywood
General Manager
Diane Borger
Finance Director
Donna Munday
Casting
Lisa Makin
Julia Horan
Marketing & Advertising
Stuart Buchanan
Emily Smith
McCabes (0171 412 2000)
Press Representation
Giselle Glasman (0171 565 5011)

Chief Electrician
Jon Such
Deputy Electrician
Michael Blim
Board Operator
Emily Brougham
Master Carpenter
Terry Bennett
Deputy Carpenter
Tim Williams
Wardrobe Master
Neil Gillies

Theatre Manager
Amanda Murray
Deputy Theatre Manager
Juliet Hayes
Duty House Manager
Gini Woodward

Box Office Manager
Terry Cooke
Deputy Box Office Manager
Tony Lee
Box Office Staff
Grainne Gillis
Laura-Kate Gordon
Jane Parker
Andrew Stevenson
Lynne Tilbury

Stage Door
Charlotte Grimes

Cleaners
Ridgeway Cleaning Services
Firemen
Myriad Security Services

ROYAL COURT THEATRE PRODUCTIONS

Royal Court Theatre Productions was formed to expand the work of the English Stage Company in the West End, with any profits covenanted to support future productions at the Royal Court Theatre at Sloane Square.

Previous productions include Serious Money by Caryl Churchill (Wyndham's Theatre, 1987), Our Country's Good by Timberlake Wertenbaker (Garrick Theatre, 1989), Death and the Maiden by Ariel Dorfman (Duke of York's Theatre, 1992), Six Degrees of Separation by John Guare (Comedy Theatre, 1992), Oleanna by David Mamet (Duke of York's Theatre, 1994), My Night With Reg by Kevin Elyot (Criterion Theatre, 1994), Rat in the Skull by Ron Hutchinson (Duke of York's Theatre, 1995), Hysteria by Terry Johnson (Duke of York's Theatre, 1995), The Changing Room by David Storey (Duke of York's Theatre, 1996).

Directors
Stuart Burge CBE
Anthony Burton
Graham Cowley
Harriet Cruickshank
Stephen Daldry
Robert Fox
Sir John Mortimer CBE QC
Sonia Melchett
Alan Rickman
Max Stafford-Clark
James L. Tanner
Company Secretary
Vikki Heywood

Photo: Juliet Stevenson and Michael Byrne in Death and The Maiden (1982), Duke of York's Theatre. Photography by Stuart Morris.

AMBASSADOR THEATRE GROUP

The Company has three main areas of activity: the operation and ownership of theatres and entertainment buildings; theatre production, particularly in the West End but also nationally and internationally; and development of new work. The Ambassador Theatre Group owns the Duke of York's and Ambassador Theatres in the West End of London. Other entertainment buildings include the Ambassadors, Woking, consisting of two theatres, including the 1,350 seat New Victoria and a six screen state-of-the-art cinema multiplex, the new 1600 seat Regent Theatre and 1400 seat Victoria Concert Hall in Stoke-on-Trent, the Milton Keynes Theatre and Theatre Royal Brighton. The Ambassador Theatre Group's co-productions include, in London, the highly acclaimed Royal Court Classics Season, comprising Ron Hutchinson's *Rat in the Skull*, David Storey's *The Changing Room*, and Terry Johnson's *Hysteria*; *Slava's Snowshow* at the Old Vic and in North America, the current 25th Anniversary production of the *Rocky Horror Show*, the national U.K. and European production of *Smokey Joe's Cafe* and the broadway production of *The Weir*. They have also recently launched a season of new plays at the New Ambassadors Theatre which included two co-productions with the Royal Court.

Board
Chairman
Sir Eddie Kulukundis OBE
Deputy Chairman
Peter Beckwith
Managing Director
Howard Panter
Executive Directors
Rosemary Squire
David Beresford Jones
Miles Wilkin

CRITERION PRODUCTIONS PLC

Criterion Productions was launched in December 1993 by Lord Attenborough and Sally Greene. The initial production was the Laurence Olivier Award-nominated production of *Jack* starring Nicol Williamson which opened at the Criterion Theatre in June 1994. Its second production was Ronald Harwood's *Taking Sides* starring Daniel Massey which played at the Criterion Theatre to great acclaim in 1995/6. This was closely followed by Harold Pinter's *The Hothouse* at the Comedy Theatre which starred the author and like *Taking Sides* was presented in association with Duncan C Weldon. Criterion Productions plc has also produced a tour of Peter Nichols' *Private's On Parade* and *Cyrano de Bergerac* at the Lyric Theatre starring Antony Sher, in association with The Royal Shakespeare Company.

Criterion Productions plc have participated in the following shows: *A Delicate Balance* starring Maggie Smith, *Closer* by Patrick Marber in the West End and Broadway, *Black Comedy* and *The Real Inspector Hound* at the Comedy Theatre, the Broadway productions of *The Judas Kiss* starring Liam Neesom, *The Blue Room* starring Nicole Kidman, *Amy's View* starring Dame Judi Dench, and *The Weir*. Criterion Productions plc was set up to allow people from all walks of life the chance to become involved with the best professional theatre productions through a small one-off investment. We are proud to have 256 shareholders and would like to thank each and every one of them.

The producers of *The Weir* wish to acknowledge financial support received from The Theatre Investment Fund, a registered charity, which invests in many commercial productions, runs seminars for new producers and raises money for the commercial theatre. If you love the theatre and wish to promote its future, please consider making a gift to the Fund. For further information regarding the Fund and its activities, please contact: Chief Executive, Theatre Investment Fund Limited, The Palace Theatre, Shaftesbury Avenue, W1V 8AY. Telephone 0171 287 2144

Original production supported by the Jerwood Foundation

FOR THE ROYAL COURT

Royal Court Theatre
Sloane Square, London SW1W 8AS
Tel: 020 7565 5050 Fax: 020 7565 5001
info@royalcourttheatre.com
www.royalcourttheatre.com

ARTISTIC

Artistic Director **Ian Rickson**
Director **Stephen Daldry**
Assistant to the Artistic Director **Jo Luke**
Associate Directors
Dominic Cooke
Elyse Dodgson
James Macdonald *
Max Stafford-Clark *
Richard Wilson *
Trainee Director **Dawn Walton****
Associate Director Casting **Lisa Makin**
Casting Assistant **Julia Horan**
Literary Manager **Graham Whybrow**
Literary Assistant **Daisy Heath**
Literary Associate **Stephen Jeffreys ***
Resident Dramatist **Simon Stephens +**
Voice Associate **Patsy Rodenburg**
International Administrator **Natalie Highwood**

YOUNG WRITERS' PROGRAMME

Associate Director **Ola Animashawun**
General Manager **Aoife Mannix**
Writers' Tutor **Nicola Baldwin**

PRODUCTION

Production Manager **Paul Handley**
Assistant Production Manager **Sue Bird**
Production Assistant **Rebecca Fifield**
Company Stage Manager **Cath Binks**
Head of Lighting **Johanna Town**
Deputy Electrician **Marion Mahon**
Assistant Electrician **Simon Lally**
Lighting Board Operator TD **Andrew Taylor**
Head of Stage **Martin Riley**
Stage Deputy **David Skelly**
Stage Chargehand **Eddie King**
Head of Sound **Paul Arditti**
Sound Deputy **Rich Walsh**
Sound Operator **Emma Laxton**
Head of Wardrobe **Iona Kenrick**
Wardrobe Deputy **Suzanne Duffy**
Maintenance Manager **Fran Mcelroy**

ENGLISH STAGE COMPANY

President **Greville Poke**
Vice Presidents **Jocelyn Herbert**
Joan Plowright CBE
Council
Chairman **Sir John Mortimer QC, CBE**
Vice-Chairman **Anthony Burton**
Members
Stuart Burge CBE
Martin Crimp
Judy Daish
Stephen Evans
Phyllida Lloyd
Baroness McIntosh
Sonia Melchett
James Midgley
Richard Pulford
Hugh Quarshie
Nicholas Wright
Alan Yentob

MANAGEMENT

Executive Director **Vikki Heywood**
Assistant to the Executive Director **Karen Curtis**
General Manager **Diane Borger**
Finance Director **Donna Munday**
Finance Officer **Rachel Harrison**
Re-development Finance Officer **Neville Ayres**

MARKETING

Head of Marketing **Stuart Buchanan**
Press Officer **Giselle Glasman**
Marketing Officer **Emily Smith**
Press Assistant **Claire Christou**
Box Office Manager **Neil Grutchfield**
Deputy Box Office Manager **Valli Dakshinamurthi**
Duty Box Office Manager **Glen Bowman**
Box Office Sales Operator **Carol Prichard,**
Gregory Woodward

DEVELOPMENT

Head of Development **Helen Salmon**
Development Associate **Susan Davenport ***
Appeals Officer **Sophie Hussey**
Administrative & Research Assistant **Olivia Hill**

FRONT OF HOUSE

Theatre Manager **Lucy Dusgate**
Deputy Theatre Manager **Jemma Davies**
Relief Duty House Manager **Grainne Cook***
Bookshop Manager **Del Campbell**
Bookshop Assistant **Sarah Mclaren ***
Stage Door/Reception **Andrew Mcloglan, Tyrone**
Lucas, Sophie Fox*, Simon David*
Thanks to all of our ushers

* part-time
+ Arts Council Resident Dramatist
** recipient of a bursary from the Arts Council of England

THE WEIR

A Nick Hern Book

This revised edition of *The Weir* first published in Great Britain
in 1994 as a paperback original by Nick Hern Books Limited,
14 Larden Road, London W3 7ST, in association with
the Royal Court Theatre, *The Weir* first published in a volume
with *St Nicholas* by Nick Hern Books in 1997

Reprinted with new front matter 1998

Typeset by Country Setting, Woodchurch, Kent TN26 3TB
Printed and bound in Great Britain by Cox and Wyman Ltd,
Reading, Berks

ISBN 1 85459 468 0

A CIP catalogue record for this book is available from the
British Library

Characters

JACK, *fifties.*
BRENDAN, *thirties.*
JIM, *forties.*
FINBAR, *late forties.*
VALERIE, *thirties.*

The play is set in a rural part of Ireland, Northwest Leitrim or Sligo. Present day. Stage setting: a small rural bar:

A counter, left, with three bar taps. The spirits are not mounted, simply left on the shelf. There are three stools at the counter.

There is a fireplace, right. There is a stove built into it. Near this is a low table with some small stools and a bigger, more comfortable chair, nearest the fire. There is another small table, front, with a stool or two.

On the wall, back, are some old black and white photographs; a ruined abbey; people posing near a newly erected ESB weir; a town in a cove with mountains around it.

An old television is mounted up in a corner. There is a small radio on a shelf behind the bar.

A door, right, is the main entrance to the bar. A door, back, leads to the toilets and a yard.

This bar is part of a house and the house is part of a farm.

The door, right, opens. JACK comes in. He wears a suit which looks a bit big for him, and a white shirt open at the collar. Over this is a dirty anorak. He takes the anorak off and hangs it up. He wipes his boots aggressively on a mat.

He goes behind the counter. He selects a glass and goes to pour himself a pint of stout. Nothing comes out of the tap. He vainly tries it again and looks underneath the counter. He turns and takes a bottle from the shelf, awkwardly prising off the top. He pours it and leaves it on the bar to settle. He turns to the till which he opens with practised, if uncertain, ease. He takes a list of prices from beside the till and holds a pair of spectacles up to his face while he examines it. He puts money in the till and takes his change.

As he finishes this, the door at back opens. BRENDAN comes in. He wears a sweater, heavy cord pants and a pair of slip-on shoes. He carries a bucket with peat briquettes. He goes to the fireplace, barely acknowledging JACK, just his voice.

BRENDAN. Jack.

JACK. Brendan. (*Lifting glass.*) What's with the Guinness?

BRENDAN (*putting peat in the stove*). I don't know. It's the power in the tap. It's a new barrel and everything.

JACK. Is the Harp one okay?

BRENDAN. Yeah.

JACK. Well, would you not switch them around and let a man have a pint of stout, no?

BRENDAN. What about the Harp drinkers?

JACK (*derision*). 'The Harp drinkers.'

BRENDAN. Your man's coming in to do it in the morning. Have a bottle.

JACK. I'm having a bottle. (*Pause.*) I'm not happy about it, now mind, right? But, like.

They laugh.

BRENDAN. Go on out of that.

JACK (*drinks*). What the hell. Good for the worms.

BRENDAN. I'd say you have a right couple of worms, alright.

They laugh. Pause. BRENDAN *stands wiping his hands.*

BRENDAN. That's some wind, isn't it?

JACK. It is.

BRENDAN. Must have been against you, was it?

JACK *comes out from behind the counter.*

JACK. It was. It was against me 'til I came around the Knock. It was a bit of shelter then.

BRENDAN *goes in behind the counter. He tidies up, dries glasses.*

BRENDAN. Yeah it's a funny one. It's coming from the North.

JACK. Mm. Ah, it's mild enough though.

BRENDAN. Ah yeah. It's balmy enough. (*Pause.*) It's balmy enough.

JACK. Were you in Carrick today?

BRENDAN. I wasn't, no. I had the sisters over doing their rounds. Checking up on me.

JACK. Checking their investments.

BRENDAN. Oh yeah. 'Course, they don't have a fucking clue what they're looking for, d'you know? They're just vaguely . . . you know.

JACK. Keeping the pressure on you.

BRENDAN. This is it. (*Pause.*) At me to sell the top field.

JACK. You don't use it much.

BRENDAN. No. No I don't. Too much trouble driving a herd up. But I know they're looking at it, all they see is new cars for the hubbies, you know?

JACK. Mm. You're not just trying to spite them? Get them vexed, ha?

BRENDAN. Not at all. I'm, just. It's a grand spot up there. Ah, I don't know. Just . . .

Short pause.

JACK. They over the whole day?

BRENDAN. They got here about two. They'd gone for lunch in the Arms. Got their story straight. Ah they were gone and all about half four.

JACK. They've no attachment to the place, no?

BRENDAN. No they don't. They look around, and it's . . . 'Ah yeah . . . ' you know?

They laugh a little.

BRENDAN. It's gas.

JACK. Mm.

BRENDAN. Were you in Carrick yourself?

JACK. I was. Flew in about eleven, threw on a fast bet. Jimmy was there, we went for a quick one in the Pot.

BRENDAN. How is he? And the ma?

JACK. Ah. Jimmy. Be in tonight. He put me on to a nice one. We got her at eleven to four.

BRENDAN. You're learning to listen, ha?

JACK. Ah. Fuck that sure. I know, but I've been having the worst run of shit you wouldn't believe. I was that desperate, I'd listen to anybody.

BRENDAN. Go on out of that.

JACK. Ah no. No no. Fair dues. I'll say it. He got us a right one. And it's good, you know. Break a streak like that.

BRENDAN. You're a user.

JACK (*laughs*). There's worse.

BRENDAN. Yeah. There might be.

JACK. But, ah, he was telling me. Did you know about Maura Nealon's house?

BRENDAN. No.

JACK. Well. Jim says he met Finbar Mack down in the Spar. Finally, either sold or's renting the, the thing, after how many years it's sat there?

BRENDAN. Jays, four or five in anyway.

JACK. Jim says five this month. And Finbar's going bananas with the great fella that he is. Patting himself on the back, goodo, and talking about the new resident. Who, he says, is a fine girl. Single. Down from Dublin and all this. And Finbar's nearly leaving the wife just to have a chance with this one. Only messing, like. But he's bringing her in here tonight, the nearest place. To old . . . Maura's. Bringing her in for a drink. Introduce her to the natives.

BRENDAN. The dirty bastard. I don't want him using in here for that sort of carry on. A married man like him.

JACK. Ah he's only old shit. He wouldn't have the nerve. Sure, how far'd he get anyway? The fucking head on him. He's only having a little thrill. Bringing her around. And I'll tell you what it is as well. He's coming in here with her. And he's the one. He's the one that's 'with' her, in whatever fucking . . . sense we're talking about. He's bringing her in. And there's you and me, and the Jimmy fella, the muggins's, the single fellas. And he's the married fella. And he's going 'Look at this! There's obviously something the fuck wrong with yous. Yous are single and you couldn't get a woman near this place. And look at me. I'm hitched. I'm over and done with, and I'm having to beat them off.'

BRENDAN. Yeah. That's the way cunts always go about their business. It's intrusive, it's bad manners, it's . . .

JACK. Ah, it's a juvenile carry on. You know?

BRENDAN. Mm.

JACK. Let her come in herself.

BRENDAN. Yeah. That'd be better. That'd make more sense, for fuck's sake.

JACK. Leave her be. Don't know if I'll stay actually.

BRENDAN. Mm.

Pause. JACK *drains his glass and puts it on the bar.*

JACK. Go on.

BRENDAN *takes the glass and pours a fresh bottle.*

JACK. Don't want to leave Jimmy in the lurch. You know? Trying to hold his own in the Finbar Mack world of big business.

They laugh a little.

BRENDAN. Fucking . . . Jimmy talking all that crack with Finbar.

JACK. That's the thing though. The Jimmy fella's got more going on up here (*Head.*) than popular opinion would give him credit for.

BRENDAN. Sure, don't we know too well for God's sake?

JACK. I know.

BRENDAN. We know only too well.

JACK *counts change out on the bar.*

JACK. Would you give us ten Silk Cut please, Brendan?

BRENDAN. Red?

JACK. Please.

BRENDAN *puts the cigarettes on the bar.*

JACK. Good man.

Pause. JACK *doesn't touch them yet.* BRENDAN *counts the money off the bar.* JACK *pauses before drinking.*

JACK. Are we right?

BRENDAN. Close enough. Cheers.

JACK. Good luck.

JACK takes a long drink. Pause.

JACK. I know I do be at you. I'll keep at you though.

BRENDAN. About what?

JACK. Don't be messing. Come on.

BRENDAN. Ah.

JACK. A youngfella like you. And this place a right going concern.

BRENDAN. Ah. The odd time. You know, the odd time I'd think about it.

JACK. You should though.

BRENDAN. Well then, so should you.

JACK. Would you go on? An auldfella like me!

BRENDAN. Would you listen to him?

JACK. Sure what would I want giving up my freedom?

BRENDAN. Well then me as well!

Pause.

JACK. Tch. Maybe. Maybe there's something to be said for the old independence.

BRENDAN. Ah there is.

Pause.

JACK. A lot to be said for it.

BRENDAN. Mm. (*Pause.*) Mm.

JACK. Cheers.

BRENDAN. Good luck.

JACK takes a long drink. The main door opens and JIM enters. He takes off an anorak to reveal a festive looking cardigan. JACK pretends not to notice him.

JACK (*winks*). Oh yes, Brendan, the luck is changing. I got me and the Jimmy fella on to a nice one today. That fella'd want to listen to me a bit more often, I tell you.

JIM. I'm going to have to start charging you for tips, am I?

JACK. Ah James! What'll you have?

JIM. Teach you some manners. Teach him some manners Brendan, ha? Small one please, Jack.

BRENDAN. Small one.

JACK. Sure it'd take more than money to put manners on me, ha Brendan?

BRENDAN. It'd take a bomb under you.

JACK. Now you said it. Bomb is right. That wind still up, Jim?

JIM. Oh it is, yeah. Warm enough though.

JACK. We were just saying.

BRENDAN. For a Northerly.

JIM. Oh that's from the West now.

BRENDAN. Is it?

JIM. Oh yeah that's a Westerly.

JACK. Must've shifted.

JIM. Mm.

Pause. JIM *comes to the bar.*

JIM. Thanking you.

JACK. Good luck.

JIM. Good luck.

BRENDAN. Good luck.

JACK *counts change out on the bar.*

JACK. Are we right?

BRENDAN *counts and pushes a coin back towards* JACK.

BRENDAN (*gathering coins*). Now we are. Sure it's hard enough to come by without giving it away.

JACK. This is it. Oh (*To* JIM.) Are you doing anything tomorrow?

JIM. What time?

JACK. I have to get out to Conor Boland. His tractor's packed up. And I have Father Donal's jalopy in since Tuesday. Said I'd change the oil. Haven't done it yet. Would you ever come in and do it so I can get over to Boland's?

JIM. It'd have to be early. I'm dropping the mother out to Sligo.

JACK. Well, whatever. Is that alright?

JIM. Ah, it should be, yeah. Pint?

JACK. Not for the moment. You go on.

JIM. Pint please Brendan. You on the bottles?

BRENDAN *takes a glass and pours* JIM *a pint of lager from the good tap.*

JACK. Ah. Medicinal.

JIM. Ha?

BRENDAN. Ah the tap's fucked.

JIM. I was wondering, 'Jaysus what's your man fucking doing now', you know?

BRENDAN. Yeah. He'd be the fella'd have a figary and be only drinking bottles from now on. He would. (*To* JACK.) You would. Be you to a fucking tee.

JACK sits as though he has to bear the world with great patience. They laugh. Pause. JACK shakes his head.

JACK. How's the mammy today?

JIM. Ah, you know?

JACK. Tch. I have to get down and see her. I keep saying it.

JIM (*tone of 'No rush. No pressure'*). Well whenever, whenever you want.

BRENDAN. Do you think you'll do anything?

JIM. About?

BRENDAN. About up there on your own and all that?

JIM. Ah. Sure where would I go? And I was talking to Finbar Mack. Be lucky to get twenty thousand for the place. Sure where would you be going with that? (*Short pause.*) You know?

JACK. With the acre?

JIM. Ah yeah, the whole . . . the whole thing.

JACK. Ah you're grand with the few little jobs around here.

JIM. Ah.

JACK. You'll be cosy enough.

Pause.

BRENDAN. Jack was telling me about Finbar. And the new eh . . .

JIM. Mmm, yeah. I was telling him earlier.

JACK. I was telling him.

JIM. I've seen her since.

BRENDAN. Oh yeah?

JIM. Yeah, they were in Finbar's car going up the Head.

JACK and BRENDAN exchange a look.

BRENDAN. Fucking hell.

JACK. Like a courting couple or something.

JIM. He's showing her the area.

JACK. Jesus. 'The area.' He's a terrible fucking thick. What the fuck, is he, doing? You know?

JIM. Ah. She's . . . This is the only place near to her.

JACK. She can . . . (*Nodding.*) find her own way surely, Jim, come on.

BRENDAN. Well it's, you know. If it's courtesy, which is one thing, and a business . . . act or whatever, you know, you have to say, well okay and . . . But if it's all messy, I'm trapped in here behind this fucking thing. And you wish he'd stop acting the mess. I have to respect whatever, they're . . .

JACK. Well this is it, we're here.

JIM. It's probably not really anything.

Short pause.

JACK. What age would she be, about, Jim?

JIM. Em. I only saw her for a sec. I'd say, (*Beat.*) like they were in the car and all. I'd say about thirties. Very nice looking.

Pause.

JACK. Dublin woman.

JIM. Dublin.

Short pause.

BRENDAN. She's no-one in the area, no?

JIM. No she's . . . coming down, you know?

JACK. Mm. (*Pause.*) Yeah.

JIM. Good luck. (*Drinks.*)

JACK. Cheers. (*Drinks.*)

BRENDAN. Good luck, boys.

JACK. Another week or two now, you'll be seeing the first of the Germans.

BRENDAN. Mm. Stretch in the evening, yeah.

JACK. You still wouldn't think about clearing one of the fields for a few caravans.

BRENDAN. Ah.

JACK. The top field.

BRENDAN. Ah there wouldn't be a lot of shelter up there, Jack. There'd be a wind up there that'd cut you.

JIM. D'you know what you could do? The herd'd be grand up there, and you could, you know, down here.

BRENDAN. Ah. (*Short pause.*) They do be around anyway. You know yourself.

JIM. Ah, they do.

JACK. You're not chasing the extra revenue.

BRENDAN. Or the work!

JIM. They do be around right enough.

BRENDAN. I'll leave the campsites to Finbar, ha? He'll sort them out.

JACK. Ah, Finbar's in real need of a few shekels.

They laugh.

BRENDAN. Ah he's in dire need of a few bob, the poor fella, that's right, that's right.

JACK. Mm.

Pause.

BRENDAN. Yeah. If you had all . . . the families out there. On their holliers. And all the kids and all. You'd feel the evenings turning. When they'd be leaving. And whatever about how quiet it is now. It'd be fucking shocking quiet then. (*Short pause.*) You know?

Pause.

JACK. Mm.

JIM. D'you want a small one, Jack?

JACK. Go on.

JIM. Two small ones please, Brendan.

BRENDAN. The small fellas.

BRENDAN *works.* JIM *counts some change on to the bar.*

JACK. Are you having one yourself?

BRENDAN. I'm debating whether to have one.

JACK. Ah have one and don't be acting the mess.

BRENDAN. Go on then.

BRENDAN *pours himself a glass of whiskey.*

JACK. Good man. (*Counts change on to the bar.*) A few shekels, ha? (*They smile.*) Mm.

JACK *takes out his cigarettes.*

JACK. Jim?

JIM. Oh cheers Jack.

JIM *takes one.*

JACK. Brendan?

BRENDAN. Fags and all, ha?

JACK. Go on. They're good for you.

BRENDAN (*taking one*). Go on.

They light up from a match which JACK *strikes. They puff contentedly for a moment.*

JIM (*lifting glass*). Keep the chill out.

JACK. This is it. Cheers.

BRENDAN. Cheers men.

JIM. Good luck.

They drink.

JACK. Now.

JIM. D'yous hear a car?

Pause.

BRENDAN. No.

JIM. That's Finbar's car.

Pause.

JIM. He's parked.

JACK. I didn't see the lights.

JIM. He came around the Knock.

From off they hear FINBAR's *voice.*

FINBAR (*off*). Ah yeah, sure half the townland used to nearly live in here.

JACK. There we are now.

The door opens and FINBAR *brings* VALERIE *in.*

FINBAR. That's it now.

FINBAR *wears a light cream coloured suit and an open collar.* VALERIE *wears jeans and a sweater. She carries a jacket.*

FINBAR. Men. This is Valerie. She's just moved into Maura Nealon's old house.

JACK. Hello, how are you?

JACK *shakes her hand.*

VALERIE. Hello.

FINBAR. This is Jack Mullen. He has a little garage up around the Knock.

JACK *nods politely.*

JACK. Now.

FINBAR. This is Jim Curran. Does a bit of work with Jack.

VALERIE *shakes hands with* JIM.

VALERIE. Pleased to meet you.

JIM. Pleased to meet you.

FINBAR. And this Brendan. Brendan Byrne.

VALERIE. Hello.

They shake hands.

BRENDAN. How are you?

FINBAR. This is his bar. And all the land I showed you. All back down the hill. That's all his farm.

VALERIE. Oh right. It's all lovely here.

BRENDAN. Oh yeah. It's a grand spot all along . . . for going for a walk or that, all down the cliffs.

FINBAR. Oh it's lovely all around here. What'll you have?

BRENDAN. Oh, I'll get this, Finbar. No. What, what do you want?

FINBAR. Oh now, ha ha. Eh, I'll have a pint then, what?, says you, if it's going, ha? Eh Harp please Brendan.

    JACK *looks at* FINBAR. FINBAR *nods at him.*

FINBAR. Jack.

JACK. Finbar.

BRENDAN. What would you like, Valerie?

VALERIE. Em. Could I have . . . Do you have . . . em, a glass of white wine?

    Pause.

BRENDAN (*going*). Yeah. I'm just going to run in the house.

VALERIE. Oh no. Don't. Don't put yourself to any trouble.

BRENDAN. No. No it's no trouble. I have a bottle.

    BRENDAN *goes.*

FINBAR. He probably has a bottle of the old vino, from feckin . . . Christmas, ha?

JACK. It's not too often the . . . the . . . wine does be flowing in here.

VALERIE. I'm all embarrassed now.

FINBAR. Don't be silly. Sit up there now, and don't mind us. Don't mind these country fellas.

JACK. Jays. You're not long out of it yourself, says the man, ha?

FINBAR (*winks*). They're only jealous Valerie because I went the town to seek my fortune. And they all stayed out here on the bog picking their holes.

JACK. Janey, now, ha? You didn't have very far to seek. Just a quick look in Big Finbar's will, I think is more like it.

FINBAR. Big Finbar's will! That's shrewd investment, boy. That's an eye for the gap.

JACK. Yeah, he probably fleeced you on Maura Nealon's house, did he?

VALERIE. I have to say I don't think so.

FINBAR. Good girl.

VALERIE. But it's very reasonable all around here, isn't it?

FINBAR. Oh it is, yeah. You know . . .

Short pause.

JACK. Is there much doing up on it?

FINBAR. Ah, hardly any.

VALERIE (*checking with* FINBAR). There's one or two floor-boards. Bit of paint.

JACK (*indicating* JIM). Well, there's your man. If you're looking for a good pair of hands.

VALERIE. Is that right?

JIM. I'll have a look for you, if you like. I know that house.

FINBAR. Don't be charging her through the nose now.

JIM. Ah ha, now.

BRENDAN *returns with a bottle of wine.*

FINBAR. You'd want to be giving her a neighbourly . . . rate, now, is the thing, ha?

JIM. Oh yeah.

JACK. Would you listen to him? 'Neighbourly rates . . . ' Wasn't by giving neighbourly rates you bought half the fucking town.

FINBAR. Half the town! (*To* VALERIE, *winking.*) I bought the whole town. Eye for the gap, you see.

JACK. Eye for your gap is right.

FINBAR (*to* BRENDAN). How long has that been in there? Lying in some drawer . . .

BRENDAN (*corkscrewing the bottle*). Ah, it was a . . . present or some . . . (*Looks at label.*) 1990. Now. Vintage, ha?

They laugh.

I hope it's alright now.

VALERIE. It's grand. I won't know the difference.

They watch BRENDAN *open the bottle. He pours a tumbler-full, then holds it up to the light, then sniffs it.*

BRENDAN. I think it's alright.

FINBAR. Ah would you give the woman the feckin' thing. The tongue's hanging out of her.

Again they watch as VALERIE *takes the glass.*

VALERIE. Thanks Brendan.

They watch her drink.

VALERIE. That's gorgeous. I'm not joking now. That's lovely.

FINBAR. Good.

BRENDAN. I'm putting it in the fridge for you, Valerie. (*He does.*)

Pause. FINBAR *nods at* VALERIE, *a reassuring 'Hello'.*

FINBAR (*to* JACK *and* JIM). How d'yous do today, boys?

JACK. Are you codding me? With this fella? Eleven to four we got her at. Came down to six to four.

FINBAR. Sheer Delight, was it?

JACK. Yeah. Kenny down in the shop, the knacker. Adjusting everything how this fella's betting.

BRENDAN. Look who's talking.

JACK. Yeah right.

JIM. He hardly ever listens to me.

JACK. Well. Now . . .

FINBAR. He's too proud, Jimmy. Too proud to admit when he needs a tip off you.

JACK (*emphatically*). I . . . have . . . my policy on this. And I have my principle. I am the first one to say it about this fella. See, usually, Valerie, usually, not all the time, Jim's not too far off the mark.

FINBAR. 'Too far off the mark!' (*To* VALERIE.) He's bang on the nail.

BRENDAN *places a pint on the bar.*

FINBAR. Thanks Brendan. (*He puts his hand in his pocket.*)

JACK. Not every time. Jim.

BRENDAN *waves* FINBAR *away.*

FINBAR. Thanks, thanks a million. (*To* VALERIE.) He is.

JACK. Bang on the nail is one thing, from judgement . . . and . . . But, and Jimmy knows I don't mean anything by this, and I know because we've spoken about this before. He has a scientific approach. He studies the form. And, no offence, he has a bit of time to be doing that. He studies it Valerie, and fair play to him, right? Do you bet on horses?

VALERIE. No.

FINBAR. Good girl.

JACK. Well he, how much, Jim, would you make in a month? On the horses.

JIM. Ah it evens out Jack. Like I'm not eh . . . I don't . . .

JACK. How much was it you got that time? When Cheltenham was on that time.

JIM. Two hundred and twenty.

JACK. Two hundred and twenty pounds, Valerie, in like three days, now. Right?

JIM. Yeah but . . .

JACK. Yeah, I know, that'd be a bigger win. But he was planning for Cheltenham for weeks, Valerie, and . . . tinkering with his figures and his . . . you know. He'd be in here with the paper up on the counter there. Brendan? Before Cheltenham?

BRENDAN. Yeah.

JACK. Right? Now, but I'm more: Ah, sure, I'll have an old bet, like. Do you know that way? And that's what I do, and to tell you the truth I don't be too bothered. It's a bit of fun and that's what it should be. And so . . . I'm not going to listen to 'Do this and do that, and you'll be right.' Just to get a few bob. There's no fun in that and the principle of it, you know?

FINBAR. Ah, the principle of the thing is to win a few quid and don't be giving out.

JACK. Who's giving out? I'm not giving out. All I'm saying is that the way I go at it, the principle's not, the science. It's the luck, it's the something that's not the facts and figures of it.

FINBAR. Jaysus. And do you and Kenny get down on your knees and lash a few quick Hail Marys out before he stamps your docket or something?

JACK. Ah it's not like that. I'm not talking about that. For fuck's sake.

FINBAR. Anyway, what the hell are you talking about? You took Jimmy's tip today, and you won so what the hell are you talking about? (*To others.*) Ha?

JACK. Ah yeah but . . . now listen because . . .

The others are laughing, going 'ah' as though FINBAR *has caught* JACK *out.*

I'll tell yous. If you won't listen . . . Right? I don't have a system. And I do. I do lose a few bob every now and then. Right? So I take a little tip from Jim. And then that'll finance having a couple of bets over the next few weeks.

They laugh.

And I've been known to have one or two wins myself, as well yous know and don't forget. I have one or two.

BRENDAN. You do not. Go on out of that you chancer.

JACK. I do.

FINBAR. I'd say the last win you had was fucking Red Rum or someone.

JACK (*aside to* VALERIE). We do be only messing like this.

FINBAR. What would anyone like? Jim?

JIM. Eh, small one then, thanks, Finbar.

FINBAR. Jack? Small one? Pint? Bottle, is it? You on the bottles?

JACK. No the tap is . . . fucking . . .

FINBAR. Oh. Typical.

JACK. Ah, I'll have a small one, go on.

FINBAR. Good man. Valerie?

VALERIE. Oh no, I'm okay for the moment, thanks.

FINBAR. Are you sure? Top that up?

VALERIE. No I'm fine, honestly.

FINBAR. You're sure now?

VALERIE. No really, I'm fine.

FINBAR (*hands up*). Fair enough. We won't force you. Give us . . . eh, three small ones, Brendan. Good man. Here, are you having one?

BRENDAN (*working*). I'm debating whether to have one.

JACK. Ah, he'll have one. Go on Brendan. Who knows when the hell you'll see another drink off the Finbar fella, ha? Come on! Quick! He's all annoyed you're having one.

FINBAR (*to* VALERIE). Would you listen to him?

JACK. That fella'd peel a banana in his pocket.

JIM. Is that what it is?

They laugh.

FINBAR. First time I've been in here for ages, bringing nice company in and everything, getting this. Oh you'd have to watch the Jimmy fella. There's more going on there than he lets on. 'Is that what that is?'

BRENDAN *places the drinks on the bar.*

And look at this! Me buying the drinks like a feckin eejit. Ah it's not right. What do you think Valerie?

VALERIE. Oh it's terrible.

FINBAR. Oh, it's desperate. (*He hands* BRENDAN *a twenty pound note.*) There you go, Brendan. I wouldn't say you see too many twenties in here. With the boys, wouldn't be too often, I'd say. Cheers boys.

JACK (*to* BRENDAN). Check that. Cheers.

JIM. Good luck.

BRENDAN. Good luck now.

VALERIE. Cheers.

JACK. How did you put up with that fella showing you around?

VALERIE. Ah, he was a bit quieter today.

JACK. Well. You're seeing the real him now. And I bet you prefer the other one. We've never seen it. The quiet Finbar. This one comes out at night, you see.

VALERIE. Oh, well I was getting the history of the place and everything today.

JACK. 'The history of the place.' You were probably making it all up on the spot, were you?

FINBAR. Yeah, I was, yeah. That's why all them photographs are fake. I had them done years ago just to fool Valerie, tonight.

VALERIE (*going to the photographs*). Oh right. That's all around here, is it?

FINBAR (*going to the photographs*). That's the weir. When was that taken, Brendan?

BRENDAN. Eh, that's 1951.

FINBAR. 1951. The weir, the river, the weir em is to regulate the water for generating power for the area and for Carrick as well. (*To* BRENDAN.) That's your dad there.

BRENDAN. Yeah. I think your dad's in it too.

FINBAR. Oh he is! Valerie, look at this. That's Big Finbar now. And that's Brendan's father, Paddy Byrne. This was when the ESB opened it. Big thing around here, Brendan.

BRENDAN. Oh yeah.

VALERIE (*to* FINBAR). You look like your father. (*To* BRENDAN.) You don't.

FINBAR. He's like his mother. He's like the Mangans. Now . . . Who would you say that is there. In the shorts.

VALERIE. Is it you?

FINBAR. Would you go on? The big fucking head on that yoke! Excuse the language. That's Jack.

VALERIE. Oh my God! How old were you there, Jack?

JACK. Em. Oh I was about seven.

VALERIE. I wouldn't have said that was you.

FINBAR. You must be joking, you'd spot that big mutton head anywhere. The photographer nearly had to ask him to go home, there wasn't going to be room in the picture. Isn't that right Jack?

JACK. That's right, and your dad nearly climbing into the camera there.

FINBAR. He was a pillar of the community, Valerie. No-one had anything against him. Except headers like your man there. (*Indicating* JACK.)

JACK. That's right, Finbar. And I'm just going in here to do something up against the pillar of the community now.

JACK *goes out door at back.*

FINBAR. Jays, he's a desperate fella, that one.

VALERIE. Where was this taken?

BRENDAN. That's the view of Carrick from our top field up there.

VALERIE. It's an amazing view.

FINBAR. Oh I'd say that's probably one of the best views all around here, wouldn't it be?

BRENDAN. Oh yeah I'd say so.

JIM. Oh yeah, it would be, yeah.

FINBAR. You get all the Germans trekking up here in the summer, Valerie. Up from the campsite.

VALERIE. Right.

FINBAR. They do come up. This'd be the scenic part of all around here, you know? Em. There's what's? There was stories all, the fairies be up there in that field. Isn't there a fort up there?

BRENDAN. There's a kind of a one.

VALERIE. A fairy fort?

FINBAR. The Germans do love all this.

BRENDAN. Well there's a . . . ring of trees, you know.

FINBAR. What's the story about the fairy road that . . . Who used to tell it?

BRENDAN. Ah, Jack'd tell you all them stories.

FINBAR. There's all this around here, Valerie, the area's steeped in old folklore, and that, you know.

BRENDAN. Jack'd know . . . the what the, you'd know a few, Jim.

JIM. Ah Jack'd tell you better than me.

FINBAR (*at photograph*). That's the Abbey now.

VALERIE. Oh yeah.

FINBAR. You can see more of it there now. What was there, Brendan? When was that?

BRENDAN. Oh, back in oh, fifteen something, there was a synod of bishops all came and met there for . . . like . . . eh.

JIM. This townland used to be quite important back a few hundred years ago, Valerie. This was like the capital of the, the county, it would have been.

VALERIE. Right.

JACK *comes back in.*

FINBAR. Oh it's a very interesting place all, eh, Jack we were just saying about the, what was the story with the fairy road?

JACK. The fairy road? I go into the toilet for two minutes. I can't leave yous alone for two minutes . . .

They laugh.

FINBAR. Ah I was telling Valerie about the fort and everything. What was the story with the fairy road? Where was it?

Short pause.

JACK. Are you really interested? All the babies.

FINBAR. Ah it's a bit of fun. Tell her. Where was it?

JACK (*to* FINBAR). You're going to regret me saying this now, 'cause you know whose house it was?

FINBAR. Whose?

JACK. It was Maura Nealon's house.

FINBAR (*self-chastising, remembering*). Oh . . . Jesus.

They laugh.

JACK. You see? That's as much cop as you have now.

FINBAR. I fucking forgot it was Maura.

JACK. These are only old stories, Valerie.

VALERIE. No. I'd like to hear it.

JACK. It's only an old cod, like.

FINBAR. You're not going to be scaring the woman.

JACK. Ah it's not scary.

VALERIE. I'm interested in it.

FINBAR. You hear all old shit around here, it doesn't mean anything.

BRENDAN. This is a good little story.

JACK. It's only short. It's just. Maura . . . Nealon used to come in here in the evening, sit over there at the fire. How old was she, Jim? When she died?

JIM. Oh Jays, she would have been nearly ninety.

JACK. But she was a grand, you know, spritely kind of a woman 'til the end. And had all her . . . She was on the ball, like, you know? And she swore that this happened. When she was only a girl. She lived in that house all her life. And she had older brothers and sisters. She was the youngest. And her mother, eh . . .

JIM. Bridie.

JACK. Bridie. She was a well-known woman in the area. A widow woman. She was a bit of a character. Bit of a practical joker and that, you know? And Maura would say that when she was young, she was, Bridie was, always doing things on the older kids, hiding their . . . clothes and all this, you know? And she'd tell them old' fibs about what a certain, prospective boyfriend or girl-friend had said about them out on the road and this about coming courting or that. And she was always shouting from upstairs or this 'There's someone at the door.' She was always saying there's someone at the back door or there's someone coming up the path. You know. This. And there'd never be, anyone there. And people got used to her. That she liked her joke.

And Maura used to say that one Saturday evening back in about 1910 or 1911, the older ones were getting ready to go out for a dance or whatever was happening. And the mother, Bridie, came down the stairs and said, 'Did no-one get the door?'

And they were all, 'Oh here we go,' you know? But – Bridie came down and *opened* the door, and there was nobody there. And she didn't say anything, And she wasn't making a big thing out of it, you know? And Maura said, she was only young, but she knew there was something wrong. She wasn't cracking the jokes. And later on, when the others were all out, it was just her and her mother sittiing at the fire. And her mother was very quiet. Normally she'd send Maura up to bed, early enough, like. But Maura said she remembered this night because Bridie didn't send her up. She wanted someone with her, you see. And in those days, Valerie, as you know, there was no electricity out here.

And there's no dark like a winter night in the country. And there was a wind like this one tonight, howling and whistling in off the sea. You hear it under the door and it's like someone singing. Singing in under the door at you. It was this type of night now. Am I setting the scene for you?

They laugh.

Finbar's looking a bit edgy. You want to finish that small one, I think.

FINBAR. Don't mind my small one. You're making very heavy weather of this yarn, Jack.

JACK. Ah now, you have to enjoy it. You have to relish the details of something like this, ha?

They laugh.

So there they were, sitting there, and Bridie was staring into the fire, a bit quiet. And smiling now and again at Maura. But Maura said she could see a bit of wet in her eyes. And then there was a soft knocking at the door. Someone. At the front door. And Bridie never moved. And Maura said, 'Will I get the door, Mammy?' And Bridie said, 'No, sure, it's only someone playing a joke on us, don't mind them.' So they sat there, and there was no more knocking for a while. And, em, in those days, there was no kitchen. Where the extension is, Valerie, that was the back door and only a little latch on it, you know? And that's where the next knocking was. Very soft, Maura said, and very low down the door. Not like where you'd expect a grown man or a woman

to be knocking, up here, you know? And again Bridie was
saying, ah, it's only someone having a joke, they'll go away.
And then it was at the window. Maura couldn't see anything out
in the night, and her mother wouldn't let her go over. And then it
stopped. But when it was late and the fire went down, Bridie
wouldn't get up to get more turf for the fire. Because it was out
in the shed. So they just sat there until the others came back,
well after midnight.

VALERIE. What was it?

JACK. Well Maura said her mother never told the others, and one
day when it was only the two of them there, a priest came and
blessed the doors and the windows. And there was no more
knocking then. And it was only years later that Maura heard
from one of the older people in the area that the house had been
built on what they call a fairy road. Like it wasn't a road, but it
was a . . .

JIM. It was like a row of things.

JACK. Yeah, like a . . . From the fort up in Brendan's top field there,
then the old well, and the abbey further down, and into the cove
where the little pebbly beach is, there. And the . . . legend would
be that the fairies would come down that way to bathe, you see.
And Maura Nealon's house was built on what you'd call . . .
that . . . road.

VALERIE. And they wanted to come through.

JACK. Well that'd be the idea. But Maura never heard the knocking
again except on one time in the fifties when the weir was going
up. There was a bit of knocking then she said. And fierce load of
dead birds all in the hedge and all this, but that was it. That's the
story.

FINBAR. You're not bothered by that, are you Valerie? 'Cause it's
only old cod, you know? You hear all these around, up and down
the country.

VALERIE. Well. I think there's probably something in them. No, I
do.

JACK. Ah, there . . . might be alright. But . . . it doesn't hurt. A bit
of an old story, like. But I'll tell you what, it'd give you a thirst,
like. You know? What'll yous have?

They laugh.

Valerie, top that up.

VALERIE. Em . . .

JACK. Go on.

FINBAR. Ah she will. Brendan.

BRENDAN *puts a clean tumbler on the bar.*

VALERIE. This glass is fine.

FINBAR. Oh, country ways! Good girl.

They laugh. BRENDAN *pours wine.*

JACK. Finbar. Pint?

FINBAR. Ah. Pint. Why not, says you, ha?

JACK. Jim?

JIM. Ah.

JACK. Two pints and one of these please, Brendan.

BRENDAN. Two pints.

Pause. BRENDAN *works.*

FINBAR. Yep. Oh yeah.

JACK. Are you debating to have one yourself?

BRENDAN. I'm debating.

FINBAR. Who's winning?

BRENDAN. Ah, it's a draw. I'm going to have a glass.

FINBAR. Good man. Have two, ha?

They laugh. JACK *produces cigarettes.*

JACK. Valerie?

VALERIE. Eh, I will, thanks.

FINBAR (*pleasantly surprised*). Oh! Good girl.

JACK. Finbar?

FINBAR. No I won't thanks Jack. Haven't had one of them fellas
now, eighteen years this November.

JACK. Eighteen years, ha?

JACK *offers the pack to* BRENDAN *and* JIM *who both take one.*

FINBAR. Eighteen years. Not since I made the move. (*To*
VALERIE.) Down to . . . Carrick.

JACK. I remember this. (*Lighting cigarettes.*) Jays, you don't look
any better for it, ha?

They laugh.

FINBAR. Oh yeah? We'll see who'd look the better after a round or
two of the fisty footwork ha? And you with the lungs hanging
out your back.

JACK. Jaysus. An auldfella like me. Ten or more years between us
and you wanting to give me a few digs. Business . . . killer
instinct, is it?

FINBAR (*winks at* VALERIE). That's an eye for the gap. Exploit
the weakness.

JACK. The weakness, yeah? Because talking of the fairy road.
Didn't you have a little run in with the fairies or who was it, that
time before you went?

FINBAR. Ah, now . . . Jaysus.

JACK. Because you were very brave that time, weren't you?

FINBAR. Ah Jack, for fuck's sake.

JACK. Ah come on now. You were great that time.

FINBAR. You're a bollocks.

JACK. Well, you. You know, talking of the fairies, now you know?

FINBAR. It wasn't the fairies. It was the . . . Walsh young one having us all on. It was only a cod, sure.

JIM. She's in America now. Niamh Walsh.

BRENDAN. It was Niamh that time, yeah?

FINBAR. Ah she was a header. Looking for attention.

VALERIE. What happened?

JACK. This was the brave fella.

FINBAR. Ah stop. It was nothing.

JACK. This was a family lived up beside Big Finbar's place. The Walshes.

FINBAR. Ah they were only blow-ins, he was a guard.

VALERIE. Blow-ins like me?

FINBAR. Ah no. You know what I what I mean.

JACK. Jays, you'll be losing business with them kind of remarks, ha? Valerie will agree with me there now.

They laugh.

FINBAR. Ah she knows what I mean. Valerie's very welcome. She knows that, don't you?

JACK. Ah leave her alone, you're embarrassing everybody now. Jaysus.

They laugh.

Tell her the story.

FINBAR. Ah Janey. Sure you have her in a haunted house already! She won't be able to sleep.

VALERIE. No. I'd like to hear it.

FINBAR. It's not even a real one.

JACK. Ah, she wants to hear one, don't be moaning and tell her, come on.

FINBAR. Tch. Just a crowd of headbangers is all it was. There was a house out near where we were on the other side of the Knock there. It would have been the nearest place to us, Valerie, about a quarter mile down the road. And the old lad Finnerty, lived on his own down there, and his family got him into a nursing home out by them down in Westport. And the people who moved in were the Walshes, and your man was a sergeant in the guards, stationed in Carrick. And, like he was fifty-odd and still only a sergeant, so, like, he was no Sherlock Holmes. You know?

They laugh.

He wasn't 'Walsh of the Yard' or anything like that. And they moved in. He had three daughters who were teenagers, and a youngfella who was married back near Longford there. So the . . . daughters were with him and the missus. And I knew them a little bit because that was the year Big Finbar died, God rest him, and they arrived about the time of the funeral so . . . you know, I met them, then. And I was living on my own because me and Big Finbar were the only two in it at that time. So I was the bachelor boy, and a gaggle of young ones after moving in next door. Yo ho! You know?

They laugh.

And around that time I would have been wondering what to do, Valerie, do you know? Whether to sell it on or farm it or, you know. I was twenty-two, twenty-three, you know? And it was, it would have been around eleven or twelve o' clock this night and there was a knock at the door and it was Mrs. Walsh. And she was all upset and asking me if I could come in, she didn't know what to do. The husband was at work, out on a call, and she didn't know anyone in the area, and there was a bit of trouble. So 'What kind of trouble?' I says. And she says she was after getting a phone call from the young one, Niamh, and she was after doing the Luigi board, or what do you call it?

VALERIE. Ouija board.

FINBAR. Ouija board.

JACK. 'Luigi board!' She was down there in the chipper in Carrick, was she, Finbar?

FINBAR. Ah fuck off. I meant the Ouija board. You know what I meant. She was after being down in . . .

JACK. 'The Luigi board.'

FINBAR. She was after, come on now, she was after being down in a friend of hers' house or this. And they were after doing the . . . Ouija board. And she phoned her mother to come and collect her. They said they were after getting a spirit or this, you know, and she was scared, saying it was after her.

And I obviously just thought, this was a load of bollocks, you know? If you'll . . . excuse the language, Valerie. But here was the mother saying she'd gone and picked her up. I mean, like, sorry, but I thought it was all a bit mad. But on the way back they'd seen something, like the mother had seen it as well. Like a dog on the road, running with the car and running after it. Like there's dogs all around here, Valerie, you know? The

farmers have them. There was a big dog up there, Jack, that
Willie McDermott had that time.

JACK. Oh Jaysus, yeah, it was like a, if you saw it from the
distance, you'd think it was a little horse. It was huge.

JIM. Saxon.

FINBAR. That was it. Saxon.

JIM. It was an Irish Wolfhound. He got it off a fella in the north.

FINBAR. Yeah it was huge. You'd be used to seeing dogs all around
the place. All kinds, but they'd be tame, like. Their bark'd be
worse than their bite. So I wasn't too . . . taken with this story.
But she wanted me to come down to the house, because when
they'd got back to the house, the young one, Niamh was going
hysterical saying there was something on the stairs. Like, no-one
else could see it. But she could. And it was a, a woman, looking
at her. And Mrs. Walsh didn't know what to do. They couldn't
contact the hubbie, and would I come down? I mean, what made
her think there was anything I could do, I don't know. But she
was panicking, you know . . . So I got in the car and we went
down. And Jesus, now, I've never seen the like of it. The young
one was in . . . bits. They had a blanket around her and she was
as white, now as . . . (*Points to* JACK'S *shirt.*) as white as that.
Well whiter, because that's probably filthy.

JACK. Ha ha.

FINBAR. But I'm not messing. And she wouldn't come out of the
living room. Because she said there was a woman on the stairs.
And I said, what's the woman doing? And she said, 'She's just
looking at me.' She was terrified. Now I didn't know whether she
was after taking drugs or drink or what she was after doing. So
I says to phone for Dr. Joe in Carrick. This is Joe Dillon, Valerie,
you'd see him in the town, he still has his surgery there beside
the Spar. Very nice fella. And I got through to him, and he was
on his way, and the Niamh one was shouting at me to close the
living room door. Because I was out in the hall where the phone
was, and she could see the woman looking at her over the
bannister. Like she was that bad, now. So Mrs. Walsh phoned Fr.
Donal, got him out of bed. And fair dues, like, he came down
and sort of blessed the place a little bit. Like he'd be more
Vatican two. There wouldn't be much of all the demons or that
kind of carry-on with him.

JACK. Jaysus, sure, he'd collapse. He's like that, (*Holds up little
finger.*) Him and a demon . . .

They laugh.

FINBAR. But Dr. Joe gave her a sedative and off she went then, you
know. And we all had a little drink, and poor Mrs. Walsh was
understandably, very, you know, shaken and everything. But Fr.
Donal told her not to mind the Ouija, and it was only an old cod.

And it was Niamh's imagination and all this. And then the phone rang, right? And it was the youngfella, the brother who was married back in Longford. And he was all, that his baby was crying and he had it out of the cot and he was standing at the window and there was all this commotion next door. Cars in the drive and all. That an aul one who lived next door who used to mind Niamh and the other sisters when they were young and all this, who was bedridden had been found dead at the bottom of the stairs. She fallen down, and they found her. And alright, whatever, coincidence. But . . . eh, that night, at home, I was sitting at the fire having a last fag before the sack, and, Jack'd know the house, the stairs come down into the, the main room. And I had my back to it. To the stairs. And it's stupid now, but at the time I couldn't turn around. I couldn't get up to go to bed. Because I thought there was something on the stairs. (*Low laugh.*)

And I just sat there, looking at an empty fireplace. And I sat there until it got bright. I was like a boy, you know? I wouldn't move in case something saw me. You know that way. I wouldn't even light another fag. Like I was dying for one, and I wouldn't . . . mad. But when it was bright then, I was grand, you know? Obviously there was nothing there and everything, but that was the last fag I ever had. (*Short pause.*) They moved away though, then, after that, the Walshes. (*Pause.*) Yep.

VALERIE. And that was when you moved. Down to Carrick.

FINBAR. Yeah (*Nods slowly.*) Maybe that . . . had something to do with it. I don't know.

VALERIE. Mm.

JACK. Moving down into the lights, yeah?

FINBAR. Mmm. Might be. Might be, alright. Didn't want the lone-liness maybe, you know? (*Pause.*) Yous all think I'm a loolah now.

They laugh.

Ha? I'm the header says you, ha? I'm going to powder my nose I think.

FINBAR *goes out door, back.*

JACK (*calling after him*). Sure, we knew you were a headbanger. Knew that all along.

They laugh. Pause.

Yeah.

VALERIE. I'd imagine though, it can get very quiet.

JACK. Oh it can, yeah. Ah, you get used to it. Brendan.

BRENDAN. Ah yeah you don't think about it.

JACK. Me and Brendan are the fellas on our own. Jim has the mammy to look after, but we're, you know, you can come in here in the evenings. During the day you'd be working. You know, there's company all around. Bit of a community all spread around the place, like.

JIM. You can put the radio on.

Pause.

JACK. Have you got any plans or that, for . . . here?

VALERIE. Not really, I'm just going to try and have some . . .

JACK. Peace and quiet.

VALERIE. Mm.

JACK. Jaysus, you're in the right place, so, ha?

They laugh.

You're going to have a peace and quiet . . . over . . . load. Oh yeah.

BRENDAN. Sure, you can always stick the head in here. Or Jack, or me or whatever, be able to sort you out for anything.

VALERIE. Thanks. I should be okay.

JACK. You're only ten minutes up the road. And Jaysus, by the looks of things you'll have a job keeping Finbar away, ha?

VALERIE. Ah he's a dote.

JACK. Jays, I've never heard him called that before, ha? Lots of other things, never that though.

FINBAR *comes back.*

FINBAR. What have you fecking heard? What are you talking about this time, Mullen, ha? About how twenty Germans were poisoned by the drink in here, last summer. (*Winks at* BRENDAN.) Ha?

JACK. No, I'd say the Arms is the place where that kind of carry-on happens. You'd get a pint in there, now, I believe, that'd put you on your back for a fortnight.

FINBAR. Don't mind them, Valerie, they're only jealous.

VALERIE. That's probably what it is, alright.

FINBAR. You see now? At least there's one person on my side.

JACK. Yeah, right. She's only sticking up for you to make sure she gets a lift after you scaring the living daylights out of her with your insistence on spooky stories.

FINBAR. Go on. It's only headers like me get a fright like that, ha? Fecking loolahs.

They laugh. JIM *counts some money.*

JIM. Does eh . . . Is anybody?

JACK. Ah no, Jim, I'm grand, you look after yourself.

JIM. Are you sure? Valerie?

VALERIE. I'll get you one.

FINBAR. Ah no Valerie, you're . . .

JACK. No, you're alright.

FINBAR. You're the guest. You're the guest.

JIM. Will you have a small one, Finbar?

FINBAR. Eh no, Jim. Thanks very much, I'm fine for the moment, finish this pint.

BRENDAN. Small one Jim? (*Pouring whiskey.*)

JIM. Thanks Brendan. I'll eh, I'll just lash a bit of turf in that, will I?

FINBAR. Good man, Jim.

> BRENDAN *gives* JIM *his drink.* JIM *leaves money on the bar and goes to the fireplace, leaving his drink on the mantel.*

JACK. Keep the chill out, ha?

FINBAR. This is it.

> FINBAR *looks at his watch.*

VALERIE. Do you want to?

FINBAR. Ah, no, no, no. I'm just watching the time. We've a wedding tomorrow.

VALERIE. Would you be . . . directly . . . working in the hotel?

JACK. Saves him paying someone's wages.

FINBAR. Sure that's how I have it, boy. (*He winks at* VALERIE.)

JACK. We know.

FINBAR. No there's certain things I do myself on a big day. One of the first things I ever learned in the business. The importance of good stock.

VALERIE. Soup stock?

FINBAR. For the soup. For the gravy, for the sauces, ah, you use it all over the place. And it's just a little thing I do. A little ritual. In the morning, I help do the stock. What do we have from yesterday and so on. A little mad thing I do, but there you are.

VALERIE. I think that's lovely.

FINBAR. Ah, it's a little thing I do. Little superstition. These'll tell you. I'm famous for it.

JACK. It's a gimmick.

BRENDAN. Who's geting married, Finbar?

FINBAR. Do you know Nuala Donnelly? 'Nu' they call her. She used to work for me in the Arms. Declan Donnelly's girl. Gas young one.

BRENDAN. Oh yeah.

FINBAR. You used to be pals with Declan, Jim.

JIM. Poor Declan. Be dead ten years in July. God rest him. Lovely fella.

FINBAR. She's a gas young one, the daughter. 'Nu' they call her. 'Call me Nu,' she says, the first day she was working for me. Not afraid to speak up for herself or anything. Used to tell us who was having affairs and all this. She was a chambermaid, you see. She knew the couples who were being all illicit because she'd go in to do the room in the morning and the bed would be already made. The woman in the affair would have done it out of guilt, you see. Cover it all up, for herself as much as for anyone else. She's a mad young one.

VALERIE. Would you get many people using the hotel like that?

FINBAR. Not at all. I wouldn't say so. But Nuala just, you know, she's a gabber and a talker.

JIM (*at stove*). Who's she getting married to, Finbar?

FINBAR. Oh Jesus, some fella from out the country. He must be in his forties. Shame, a young one getting hitched to an auld fell like that. He must have plenty of money. (*To* VALERIE, *indicating* JACK.) Be like getting married to that. He's a nice stash hidden away in that little garage, I'll tell you. Hoping to trap some little thing with it. Isn't that right, Jack?

JACK. That's my plan.

FINBAR. But you want to be careful of the old lads living on their own. They've a big pot of stew constantly on the heat, and they just keep throwing a few bits of scraps in it every couple of days. And they'd survive on that, don't you Jack? That'd do you?

JACK. It's a feast every day.

FINBAR. Aw. Dreadful fellas. And then they manage to get a girl and the dust'd be like that on everything. And your man'd be after living in two rooms all his life, and the poor young one would have to get in and clean it all out. Thirty years of old newspapers and cheap thrillers, all lying there in the damp since their mammies died and that was the last bit of cleaning went on in the place. That right Jack?

JACK. That's us to a tee.

BRENDAN. Jaysus, speak for yourself, ha?

FINBAR. Oh, they'd be desperate men. Changing the sheets in the bed every Christmas. And there'd be soot all over everything, and bits of rasher, and egg and pudding on the floor.

VALERIE. The poor girl.

JACK. Poor girl is right. So the least I can do is make sure her reception, in the Arms, is a little memory for her to have in the future, in the cold nights. Cheers.

They have all enjoyed this.

JACK. You've a terrible warped mind, do you know that?

FINBAR (*winks at* VALERIE). Sure I'm only telling like it is, ha?

JIM. Nuala getting married. You don't feel the time.

FINBAR. No.

JIM. Mmm. I remember, oh, it must have been twenty or more
   years ago, doing a job with him. Declan. Talking about what we
   were saying earlier. The priest over in Glen was looking for a
   couple of lads to do a bit of work. And he was down in Carrick
   in the Arms. He'd, come over, from Glen, you know? Which
   was an odd thing anyway. Like what was he doing coming all
   the way over just to get a couple of young fellas? But Declan,
   Donnelly, got put on to him. There was a few quid and he
   knocked up to me and we were to go over to the church in
   Glen the following day. And I remember I was dying with the
   'flu and I had a terrible high temperature. The mother was telling
   me to stay in the leaba. Burn it off. But like it was a couple of
   quid on the QT so I told Declan yeah, I'd do it tomorrow.
   No problem.

And then the next day it was lashing rain. I'll never forget it. He
   called for me in his dad's car. The smell of sheep in it like you
   wouldn't believe. God it would kill you. He used to put them in
   the car, chauffeur them around, you know?

Smiles.

And we drove over to Glen. And the priest took us into the
   sacristy, and the job, of all things was to dig a grave in the yard.
   That day was the removal of the remains and they needed the
   grave for the morning. And fair dues, like, Declan said it to him.
   Was there no-one else around the place could have done it? And
   the priest got a bit cagey and he was saying something about the
   local boys being busy with a game of Gaa, or something. And
   the rain was pelting down and he gave us leggings and wellies
   and the whole bit they had there and a couple of shovels.

And then he put up his umbrella all annoyed, like, and he
   brought us out, over to a grave under a tree. It was a family one
   and there were two down in it already, the mother and the father
   and this was going to be for the boy. Well he was a man, like, a
   middle-aged fella. But there was two in it so we weren't going
   to have to go down for miles, like. So he went off to do his
   business and get ready, and me and Declan got stuck in. And
   with the rain and all, I was dying with the 'flu. My arms were
   sore and then my legs got sore. And then my neck got sore. And
   I was boiling. But we got down two, two and a half foot and we
   took a break. We got in Declan's car and he pulled out a bottle of
   poitin and a few sambos. I couldn't eat but I took a good belt of
   the bottle, like. Knocked me into some sort of shape. And we
   just sat there for a while, listening to the radio, and the rain

coming down, and then we got out and got stuck in again.
Having a little swig every half hour or so, keeping it going.

And we saw the hearse arrive then. And the mad thing was, there
was only two or three other fellas there for the service. Of course
the removal is only a short thing mostly, but to have no-one
there, and for a man who's not an old man, it was funny, you
know?

And then that was over and the priest came out to us. We were
nearly finished. And he just cleared us for the funeral in the
morning, and then he went off. So me and Declan were the only
two there, then. (*Short pause.*) And your man was laid out in
the church. And Declan went off to get a tarp to stretch over . . .
the . . . grave, and I put a big lump of a door over it. And I was
just waiting on Declan and having the last drop, under the tree
and thinking we might stick the head in somewhere for a quick
pint on the way back. You know?

And then I saw this, fella, come out of the church and he walked
straight over to me. He was in a suit so I reckoned he was paying
his respects or whatever. And over he comes, through the grave-
stones. And he was looking around him a bit, like he didn't know
the place. And he stood beside me, under the tree, looking at
the grave. I didn't know what to say, you know? And he goes,
'Is this for so and so?' I forget the name. And I go, 'That's right,
yeah.' And he says, 'That's the wrong grave.' And I'm like,
'No. This is where the priest said, like.' And he looked at me,
breathing hard through his nose. Like he was holding his temper.
And he goes, 'Come on, I'll show you.' And he walks off.

And I was all like 'fuck this' you know? And I was cursing
Declan, waiting for him to come back. And your man turns
around, you know, 'Come on, it's over here.' I just, he was a
loolah, you know? And I was nearly climbimg into the grave
myself, with the tiredness. And I was sick. So I followed him
just to get it over with. And he stopped at a grave. Like a new
enough one. A white one with a picture of a little girl on it.

And he says, It's this one here. And I just went, 'Okay, right
you are Mister, I'll have it done, no problem. See you now.' And
he . . . sort of touched the gravestone and he went off, back into
the church. I was breathing a few sighs of relief I'll tell you.
And Declan came back with the tarp and I said, 'Did you see
your man?' And he didn't know what I was talking about. So
I told him and all this, and we just kind of had a bit of a laugh
at it. And we just got out of there. Stopped in the Green Man on
the way back for a few pints and that night my fever broke. But
I was knackered. The mother wouldn't let me go to the burial.
Declan did it on his own I think. But I was laid up for a couple
of days. And one day the mother brought me in the paper and on
the obituaries, there was a picture of your man whose grave we'd
dug. And you know what I'm going to say. It was the spit of

your man I'd met in the graveyard. So I thought first it was a brother or a relative or someone, I'd met.

And I forgot about it a bit and didn't think about it for ages until one night Declan told me he'd found out why the priest from Glen was looking for a couple of Carrick fellas, for the job. The fella who'd died had had a bit of a reputation for em . . . being a pervert. And Jesus, when I heard that, you know? If it was him. And he wanted to go down in the grave with the . . . little girl. Even after they were gone. It didn't bear . . . thinking about. It came back when you said about Declan's girl. Yeah.

Pause.

FINBAR. Jaysus, Jim. That's a terrible story, to be telling.

JIM. Well, you know. And we'd been having the few little drinks. From Dick Lenihan's batch, you know?

JACK. Oh Jesus. Firewater. Sure that'd put a hole in the glass, let alone give you hallucinations.

A little laugh.

Pause.

VALERIE. Do you think it was a, an hallucination Jim?

JIM. God, I don't know. I was flying like, but it was a right fluke him showing me where he wanted to be buried and me knowing nothing about him like.

VALERIE. Mm. (*Nods.*)

FINBAR. Are you alright, Valerie? (*Little laugh.*) You look a bit peaky there.

VALERIE. No, I'm fine. Just, actually, is the ladies out this way?

BRENDAN. Ah. (*Short pause.*) Jays, I'll tell you what, Valerie, this is very embarrassing but the ladies is busted. And with the . . .

JACK *laughs.* BRENDAN *chuckles a little.*

I'm getting it fixed for the Germans like, but I haven't done it yet.

FINBAR. Ah, you're a terrible man, Brendan.

BRENDAN. No, I'll bring you in the house, come on.

VALERIE. Are you sure?

BRENDAN. Aw yeah, yeah, no problem.

JACK. Don't worry Valerie, if you're not back in ten minutes we'll come and get you, okay?

BRENDAN. Jaysus. Give it a rest. Come on Valerie, I'll put the lights on for you. Out this way.

FINBAR. Bye now.

VALERIE. Bye.

BRENDAN, *a little awkwardly, shepherds* VALERIE *out the back.*

Pause.

JACK. Yep.

Short pause.

FINBAR (*to* JIM). Jaysus. That's some fucking story. To be telling a girl, like. Perverts out in the country. For fuck's sake.

Short pause.

JACK. Like your story had nothing in it, ha?

FINBAR. Ah that was only old headers in it.

JACK. But you brought the whole thing up. With the fairies. The fairies! She's in that house.

FINBAR. I forgot it was that house. I forgot it was Maura Nealon. It was an honest mistake.

JACK. Honest mistake.

FINBAR. What.

JACK. Don't be giving it that old cod now.

FINBAR. What do you mean?

JACK. With bringing her around and all.

FINBAR. What about it?

JACK. Bringing her up the Head and all.

Short pause. FINBAR *looks at* JIM *and back at* JACK.

FINBAR. Yeah?

JACK. So don't be giving it the old cod now.

FINBAR. What cod, Jack? (*Pause.*) I'm asking you. (*Short pause.*) What?

JIM. Ah boys, we have a small one. Come on now.

FINBAR. Hang on a minute, Jim. What?

JACK. Well you get me to tell a story about the house she's in.

FINBAR. I didn't *know* that though. I told you that.

JACK. Whatever. And then you tell the story about the Walsh girl.

FINBAR. Sure it was you told me to say that.

JACK. What?

FINBAR. Talking about the fags and giving up the fags and all that. When you offered them that time.

JACK. Would you cop on? 'Ghosts' and 'Giving up the fags.'

FINBAR. Okay. I'm sorry. What? I regret the stories, then. I don't think we should have any more of them. But that's what I'm saying, like.

JIM. I didn't think. I just said it. With, Declan Donnelly and that. It just, you know . . .

FINBAR. Ah no no no. Jim. We're not blaming anybody. I regret it now. And let's not have any more of them, and that's all.

JACK. Oh you regret it now?

FINBAR. Yeah.

JACK. It's not part of the tour.

FINBAR. Ah now, come on.

JACK. Bit of local colour.

FINBAR. No. Jack.

JACK. Just don't berate Jim for telling a story after you telling one yourself.

FINBAR. I apologise, if that's what I did. Sorry Jim. Now, I'll say that. But stop with this . . . tour guide thing. That's not fair. The woman's moved out here on her own. For some reason. There's something obviously going on . . . in her life. I'm just trying to make it easier for her. Give her a welcome, for fuck's sake. So don't . . . be implying anything else. I don't like it. (*Pause.*) I've apologised to Jim. And I'm saying no more stories. (*Short pause.*) Sure I'm married! I mean really. Yous are the single boys. (*Short pause. Warm.*) Sure I can't remember the last time I saw a suit on you.

Pause.

JACK. Oh now it's me?

JIM. Ah now boys, come on. That's enough. That's enough of that.

JACK. You think I have intentions, is it?

FINBAR. I don't know. You're entitled.

JACK. I do often wear a suit. Don't come in here for the first time in God knows, thinking we're fucking hicks. 'Cause you're from round here.

Pause.

FINBAR. Nobody's saying that. You've got the wrong idea, Jack. And it's not worth falling out over. Now, I'll buy you a drink. And that'll be the fucking end of it now. Alright?

JACK. You will not buy me a fucking drink. (*Short pause.*) I'll buy *you* one, and *that'll* be the end of it.

JACK *extends his hand. They shake.*

JIM. That's more like it, men. That's more like it, ha?

JACK *goes in behind the bar.*

JACK. What'll yous have?

FINBAR (*offering hand to* JIM). Sorry Jim.

JIM. Ah no no no. Stop. (*Shaking hands.*) It's forgotten.

JACK. Finbar.

FINBAR. Ah. I think I'll just have a glass, Jack, I think.

JACK. Ah, you'll have a small one with that.

FINBAR. Jays, you'll fucking kill me now, ha? I think he's trying to kill me Jim, is he?

JIM. Oh now.

JACK. Jim?

JIM. Small one, Jack, thanks.

JACK. You'll have a little pint with that I think.

JIM. Go on, ha?

FINBAR. Ah good man. (*Pause.*) Jays. That was a hot one there for a minute, ha?

JACK. We'll say no more about it. We might tell a few jokes when she comes back.

They laugh.

FINBAR. Jays. This is it. How's the mammy, Jim?

JIM. Ah, do you know what it is? She's just old. And everything's going on her.

FINBAR. Ah Jaysus, ha? I'll have to get up and see her.

JACK. I was saying that earlier. It'd be the time, you think, Jim.

JIM. Ah.

FINBAR. She does be alright on her own, with coming out for an old jar or that.

JIM. Oh don't mind her. She's well able to tell you what's what. The only thing would be the eyes. But she's the one. I'm always mixing up the tablets. She knows exactly what she's supposed to be taking when. So. But we have the telly in that room. And she'll listen to that and drop off.

FINBAR. Well that's alright, isn't it.

JIM. Oh she's still . . . I'm taking her over to see her sister in the, in the order.

JACK. That's a closed order, Jim, yeah?

JIM. Yeah, you know. They don't talk and all that. But the sister is six years older than the mammy, now, you know, so . . .

FINBAR. Gas. She'll be alright for the drive?

JIM. Oh, she'll be knackered, she'll be out like a light when we get back.

FINBAR. Ah.

JIM. Ah yeah.

BRENDAN *and* VALERIE *come back.*

BRENDAN. So this was all the original. Before the house.

VALERIE. Right.

FINBAR. There you are, we thought we were going to have to send out a search party.

VALERIE. I was having a good nosy around.

FINBAR. Wasn't too much of a state, no?

.VALERIE. Tidier than I normally am.

JACK. That's he had the sisters over today. That's all that is.

FINBAR. I saw them having their lunch in my place today.

BRENDAN. Don't be talking.

FINBAR (*gingerly*). Oh . . . back off there. Sensitive area. Eh, Valerie, darling, I don't want you to be stranded here with me now if I'm keeping you.

BRENDAN. Sure we can look after her.

FINBAR. Ah no, I'm grand for a while yet.

VALERIE. I, em. Hearing about. All these . . . you know, stories. It's . . .

FINBAR. Ah that's the end of them, now. We've had enough of them old stories, they're only an old cod. We've just been joking about it there when you were out. We'll all be all be witless, ha? We won't be able to sleep in our beds!

VALERIE. No, see, something happened to me. That just hearing you talk about it tonight. It's important to me. That I'm not . . . bananas.

I mean, I'm a fairly straight . . . down the line . . . person. Working. I had a good job at DCU. I had gone back to work after having my daughter, Niamh. My husband teaches, engineering, at DCU. We had Niamh in 1988. And I went back to work when she was five, when she started school. And we'd leave her with Daniel's parents, my husband's parents. His mother always picked her up from school. And I'd collect her after work. And last year she, she was dying to learn how to swim.

And the school had a thing. They'd take the class down to the CRC in Clontarf on Wednesdays. She was learning very well. No problem. Loved the water. She couldn't wait for Wednesdays and swimming. Daniel used to take her to the pool on Saturdays and everything.

But for such a bright, outgoing, happy girl she was a big em . . . She had a problem sleeping at night. She was afraid of the dark. She never wanted you to leave the room.

One of us would have to lie there with her until she went off, and even when she did, she'd often have to come in and sleep with us.

And I'd say to her, 'What's wrong, when you go to bed?' But in the daytime, you know, she wouldn't care. Night-time was a million miles away. And she wouldn't . . . think about it. But at night . . . there were people at the window, there were people in the attic, there was someone coming up the stairs. There were children knocking, in the wall. And there was always a man standing across the road who she'd see. Like there was loads of things. The poor . . . I wanted to bring her to the doctor, but Daniel said she'd grow out of it. And we should be careful, just, about books we got her, and what she saw on the telly and all of this.

But I mean, she used to even be scared that when she got up in the morning that Mammy and Daddy would have gone away and she'd be in the house on her own. That was one she told Daniel's mother. And all the furniture and carpets and everything would be gone. I mean, you know? So I told her after that, you know, we'd never, you know, it was ridiculous. And that if she was worried at all during the day to ring me, and I'd come and get her, and there was nothing to worry about. And she knew our number, she was very good at learning numbers off and everything. She knew ours and her Nana's and mine at work. She knew them all.

But then, in March, last year, the school had a, a sponsored swim, and the kids were going to swim a length of the pool. And I promised I was going to watch her. But I got . . . I was late, out of work, and I was only going to be in time to meet her afterwards, but em, when I got there . . . There was an ambulance and I thought, like, the pool is in the Central Remedial Clinic, so I thought like it was just somebody being dropped there. I didn't really pay any attention.

But when I got in, I saw that there was no-one in the pool and one of the teachers was there with a group of kids. And she was crying and some of the children were crying. And this woman, another one of the mums came over and said there'd been an accident. And Niamh had hit her head in the pool and she'd been in the water and they'd been trying to resuscitate her. But she said she was going to be alright.

And I didn't believe it was happening. I thought it must have been someone else. And I went into, I was brought into, a room and Niamh was on a table. It was a table for table-tennis, and an ambulance man was giving her the . . . kiss of life.

She was in her bathing suit. And the ambulance man said he didn't think what he was doing was working. And he didn't know if she was alive. And he wrapped her in a towel and carried her out to the ambulance. And I got in the back with him. And they radioed on ahead, they were going to put her on a machine in Beaumont and try to revive her there. But the ambulance man knew, I think. She wasn't breathing, and he just knew, and he said if I wanted to say goodbye to her in the ambulance in case I didn't get a chance at the hospital.

And I gave her a little hug. She was freezing cold. And I told her Mammy loved her very much. She just looked asleep but her lips were gone blue and she was dead.

And it had happened so fast. Just a few minutes. And I don't think I have to tell you. How hard it was. Between me and Daniel, as well. It didn't seem real. At the funeral I just thought I could go and lift her out of the coffin and would be the end of all this.

I think Daniel was. I don't know if he actually, blamed me, there was nothing I could do. But he became very busy in his work. Just. Keeping himself . . . em. But I was, you know, I was more, just I didn't really know what I was doing. Just walking around, wanting to . . . Sitting in the house, with Daniel's mother, fussing around the place.

Just, months of this. Not really talking about it, like.

Pause.

But, and then one morning. I was in bed, Daniel had gone to work. I usually lay there for a few hours, trying to stay asleep, really. I suppose. And the phone rang. And I just left it. I wasn't going to get it. And it rang for a long time. Em, eventually it stopped, and I was dropping off again. But then it started ringing again, for a long time. So I thought it must have been Daniel trying to get me. Someone who knew I was there.

So I went down and answered it. And. The line was very faint. It was like a crossed line. There were voices, but I couldn't hear what they were saying. And then I heard Niamh. She said, 'Mammy?' And I . . . just said, you know, 'Yes.'

Short pause.

And she said . . . She wanted me to come and collect her. I mean, I wasn't sure whether this was a dream or her leaving us had been a dream. I just said, 'Where are you?'

And she said she thought she was at Nana's. In the bedroom. But Nana wasn't there. And she was scared. There were children knocking in the walls and the man was standing across the road, and he was looking up and he was going to cross the road. And would I come and get her?

And I said I would, of course I would. And I dropped the phone and I ran out to the car in just a teeshirt I slept in. And I drove to Daniel's mother's house. And I could hardly see, I was crying so much. I mean, I knew she wasn't going to be there. I knew she was gone. But to think wherever she was . . . that . . . And there was nothing I could do about it.

Daniel's mother got a doctor and I . . . slept for a day or two. But it was . . . Daniel felt that I . . . needed to face up to Niamh being gone. But I just thought that he should face up to what happened to me. He was insisting I get some treatment, and then . . . everything would be okay. But you know, what can help that, if she's out there? She still . . . she still needs me.

Pause.

JACK. You don't think it could have been a dream you were having, no?

Short pause.

VALERIE. I heard her.

Short pause.

FINBAR. Sure, you were after getting a terrible shock, Valerie. These things can happen. Your . . . brain is trying to deal with it, you know? (*Pause.*) Is your husband going to . . . come down?

VALERIE. I don't think so.

FINBAR. Ah, it'd be a terrible shame if you don't . . . if you didn't see . . . him because of something as, as, you know . . . that you don't even know what it was.

Short pause.

BRENDAN. She said she knew what it was.

FINBAR. But sure you can't just accept that, that you, you know . . . I mean . . . surely you, you have to look at the broader thing of it here.

JIM. It might have been a wrong number.

BRENDAN. What?

JIM. It could have been a wrong number or something wrong with the phone, you know? And you'd think you heard it. Something on the line.

BRENDAN. But you wouldn't hear someone's voice on the fucking thing, Jim.

JIM. Just it might have been something else.

JACK. Here, go easy, Brendan, Jim's only trying to talk about the fucking thing.

FINBAR. Ah lads.

JACK. Just take it easy.

VALERIE. Stop. I don't want . . . It's something that happened. And it's nice just to be here and . . . hear what you were saying. I know I'm not crazy.

Short pause.

FINBAR. Valerie, love, nobody's going to think that. But . . . just . . . no-one knows about these things, sure, they're not real even. You hear all sorts of old cod, all around. But there's usually some kind of explanation for it. Sure, Jim said himself he was delirious with the 'flu that time. Jim.

JIM. I had a right temperature.

FINBAR. Maura . . . eh . . . Nealon, sure she was in here every night of the week. Brendan. About how much would she drink? Be honest now.

BRENDAN. How much did she drink?

JACK. Have a bit of respect, Finbar.

FINBAR. I'm trying to make a point, Jack. The woman was a drinker.

JACK. We're all drinkers.

FINBAR. But, come on. She was an alcoholic, Valerie. She used to have a bottle of whiskey put away before you knew where you were. Sure who wouldn't be hearing knocking after that?

JACK. Ah you're not being fair on her now. The woman's dead, she can't defend herself.

FINBAR. I'm not casting anything on her. If she came in that door right now, if she was alive, I'd be buying her drink, and more power to her, I'd hope she'd enjoy it. I'd be the first to buy her a drink. But I run a bar myself down in the Arms. And I know all about what a right few drinks'll do to you. She liked her drop is what I'm saying.

BRENDAN. What about you? And the Walshes?

FINBAR. Look. How many times do I have to say it? They were all a bunch of fucking headbangers!

Pause.

I got the wind put up me that night. Fair enough. But that's what these stories do. But I resent that now. What I went through that night. But I was only young. And that's over with, fucking headbangers.

Pause.

And after all that, I'm ignoring the bigger thing. I'm very sorry about your daughter, Valerie, I'm very sorry indeed.

JACK. Oh we all are. Of course we are. It's terrible.

Long pause.

FINBAR (*checks watch*). I'm going to have to go, I'm afraid. I don't want to, but . . .

VALERIE. Okay.

BRENDAN. Ah here, I'll leave her down.

FINBAR. But you might want to come on now, no?

VALERIE. Em.

BRENDAN. Ah, have another drink and relax for a little while.

VALERIE. Yeah, I think I'm going to hang on for another little while.

FINBAR. Are you going to go easy on the old stories?

JACK. Ah stop being an old woman. She'll be grand.

FINBAR. Alright?

JACK. She'll be grand.

JIM. Could I get a lift, Finbar?

FINBAR. Of course you can, Jim.

JACK. You're okay for Father Donal's car in the morning.

JIM (*counting money*). No problem. I'll be there about quarter to nine.

JACK. Grand, just, I've got to get out to Conor Boland.

JIM. Yeah. It's fine. Brendan, em . . .

BRENDAN. Naggin?

JIM. Please.

> BRENDAN *puts a small bottle of whiskey in a plastic bag and gives it to* JIM. JIM *attempts to pay for it.* BRENDAN *discreetly waves him away.*

FINBAR. Yep.

JIM. Well. Valerie.

VALERIE. It was very nice to meet you.

JIM (*taking her hand*). I'm very sorry about what's happened to you. And I'm sure your girl is quite safe and comfortable wherever she is, and I'm going to say a little prayer for her, but I'm sure she doesn't need it. She's a saint. She's a little innocent. And that fella I saw in the churchyard that time was only the rotten poitin and the fever I had. Finbar's right. You enjoy your peace and quiet here now. And we'll see you again. You're very nice. Goodnight now.

VALERIE. Goodnight. Thanks Jim.

JIM. That's alright.

FINBAR. Valerie. (*He takes her hand.*)

VALERIE. Thanks for everything.

FINBAR. My pleasure, darling. And I'll call up to you now in the next day or two, and . . . (*Nods at her.*)

VALERIE. Fine.

FINBAR. And we'll make sure you're alright and you're settling in with us. You're very welcome.

> *He kisses her awkwardly on the cheek.*

VALERIE. Thanks for everything, Finbar.

FINBAR. That's quite alright. Men.

JACK. Finbar.

FINBAR. I'll see you soon, I hope, Jack.

They shake hands.

FINBAR. Alright?

JACK. See you soon.

FINBAR. Brendan.

BRENDAN. Take it easy now, Finbar. Look after yourself.

FINBAR. I won't leave it so long next time.

BRENDAN. Okay.

JIM. Goodnight.

BRENDAN. Goodnight Jim.

VALERIE. See you soon.

JACK. See you in the morning.

JIM. Quarter to nine.

FINBAR. See yous now.

JIM and FINBAR leave.

JACK. There you are now.

BRENDAN. Mm.

JACK. I'm sorry for snapping. That time.

BRENDAN. Ah no. Sure. I was . . .

VALERIE. I think it was my fault.

JACK. Would you go on? Of course it wasn't your fault. You know . . . It's all very well, us sitting around, fecking around with these old stories. But then, for something personal like that. That's happened to you. People are going to deal with it, in different ways. Jim, was, you know . . .

BRENDAN. Yeah . . .

JACK. He didn't mean anything.

BRENDAN. He didn't really mean there was anything wrong with your phone, I don't think.

They laugh a little. Pause.

JACK. It's em . . . a terrible thing that happened. Do you ever get over something like that, I wonder? I don't mean the phone . . . call, you know.

VALERIE. I know. (*Pause.*) I don't know. (*Pause.*)

JACK. We're very sorry.

BRENDAN. Come on we sit near the stove. It's getting cold. We'll have a last one.

JACK. Good idea.

BRENDAN. Give us your glass, Valerie. Jack, you'll have a small one, for the road.

VALERIE. Can I get this?

JACK. Ah no no no.

BRENDAN. It's on the house now. Bar's officially closed. Go on.

JACK *and* VALERIE *move nearer the stove.*

JACK. You get yourself in there now. We'll be grand in a minute.

BRENDAN. I'm going to give you a little brandy, Valerie. This wine is freezing in the fridge.

JACK. Good man.

VALERIE. Oh lovely. Thanks.

JACK. Good girl. That's it now. (*To* BRENDAN.) Jim'll be in a bad way, all the same when the mammy goes, what do you think Brendan?

BRENDAN. Oh definitely. She's been very sick, Valerie, for years now. Fading fast, like, for years! She still spoils that boy rotten, ha? Though.

JACK. Oh definitely. Oh yeah.

BRENDAN *brings the drinks over.*

VALERIE. That's an awful lot.

BRENDAN. Ah it's not really.

JACK. There's no law says you have to drink it all, ha? Your man does put it back in the bottle.

BRENDAN. Would you ever fuck off?

JACK. I think we should drink this to you, sweetheart.

BRENDAN. Yes. to Valerie.

JACK. Hope it's all . . . (*Raises glass.*) In the end . . .

BRENDAN. Cheers.

VALERIE. Cheers.

They drink. JACK *considers* BRENDAN *for a moment.*

JACK. There's the boy, ha?

They smile.

VALERIE. You've no children, Jack, no?

JACK. No, darling, never married. But I do be telling this fella to be on the lookout. A youngfella like him. Not to end up like me.

VALERIE. Do you wish you had married?

JACK. Sure who'd have me? A cantankerous old fucker like me.

BRENDAN. Too right.

JACK. Yeah . . . It's a thing, you know? I do say it to Brendan. I'm down in the the garage. And the fucking tin roof on the thing. On my own on that country road. You see it was bypassed by the main road into Carrick. And there's no . . . like in the summer the heat has the place like an oven, with the roof, or if it's not that, it's the rain pelting down on it like bricks, the noise of it. And there you'll be, the only car stopping in be someone that knows the area real well. Ah, you'd definitely feel it, like. But you know. I get down here for a pint and that. There's a lot to be said for the company. And the . . . you know, the . . . someone there. Oh yeah.

VALERIE. Did you never consider it? When you were young.

JACK. Oh sure. Yeah. Of course I did Sure what the hell else does a youngfella be thinking about? You know?

And Brendan knows. I had a girl. A lovely girl back then. We were courting for three, years, and em . . . 1963 to 66. But she wanted to go up to Dublin, you know. She would have felt that's what we should have done. And I don't know why it was a thing with me that I . . . an irrational fear, I suppose, that, kept me here. And I couldn't understand why she wanted to be running off up to Dublin, you know? And she did in the end, anyway, like. And she was working up there waiting for me to come.

But with me it was a mad thing, that I thought it was a thousand fucking miles away. Hated going up.

I went up a few times like. But . . . I was going up for . . . you know . . . she had a room. A freezing, damp place. I was a terrible fella. It became that that was the only thing I was going for. I couldn't stand being away. I don't know why. Ah, I'd be all excited about going up for the physical . . . the freedom of it. But after a day and a night, and I'd had my fill, we'd be walking in the park and I'd be all catty and bored, and moochy.

Pause.

Breaking the poor girl's heart. Ah, you get older and look back on why you did things, you see that a lot of the time, there wasn't a reason. You do a lot of things out of pure cussedness.

I stopped answering her letters. And I'd fucking dread one coming to the house. And her in it wondering how I was and was there something wrong with the post or this.

Pause.

I can't explain what carry on I was up to. I had just . . . left her out. Being the big fella, me dad handing over the business to me. Me swanning around. A man of substance. And then I had the gall to feel resentful when she wrote and said she was getting married to a fella.

Pause.

And I was all that it was her fault for going up in the first place. Tss.

There was a delegation of people from all around here going up to the wedding on a bus. And I was just one of the crowd. Just one of the guests. In my suit, and the shoes nearly polished off me. And a hangover like you wouldn't believe. I'd been up 'til five or more, swilling this stuff, looking at the fire. And we were all on the bus at nine. And all the chat all around was why she hadn't come home to get married. And me sick as a dog.

The smell of Brylcreem off all us culchies. Sitting in the church in Phibsboro. All her lovely-looking nurse friends and their guard boyfriends. She was marrying a guard. Huge fella. Shoulders like a big gorilla. And they were coming down the aisle after, and I caught her eye. And I gave her the cheeziest little grin you've ever seen. A little grin that was saying, 'Enjoy your big gorilla, 'cause the future's all ahead of me.'

And she just looked at me like I was only another guest at the wedding. And that was that. And the future *was* all ahead of me. Years and years of it. I could feel it coming. All those things you've got to face on your own. All by yourself. And you bear it 'cause you're showing everybody that you're a great fella altogether.

But I left the church like a little boy. And I walked away. I couldn't go to the reception. I just kept walking. There was a light rain. I just kept walking. And then I was in town. It was a dark day. Like there was a roof on the city. And I found myself in a little labyrinth of streets. With nothing doing. And I ducked into a pub. Little dark place. Just one or two others there. A businesslike barman. Like yourself Brendan, ha?

Businesslike, dutiful. And I put a pint or two away. And a small one or two. And I sat there, just looking down at the dirty wooden bar. And the barman asked me if I was alright? Simple little question. And I said I was. And he said he'd make me a sandwich. And I said okay. And I nearly started crying – because, you know, here was someone just . . . and I watched him.

He took two big slices off a fresh loaf and buttered them carefully, spreading it all around. I'll never forget it. And then he sliced some cheese and cooked ham and an onion out of a jar, and put it all on a plate and sliced it down the middle. And, just someone doing this for me. And putting it down in front of me. 'Get that down you now,' he said. And then he folded up his newspaper and put on his jacket and went off on his break. And there was another barman then.

And I took this sandwich up and I could hardly swallow it, because of the lump in my throat. But I ate it all down because someone I didn't know had done this for me. Such a small thing.

But a huge thing in my condition. It fortified me, like no meal I ever had in my life. And I went to the reception. And I was properly ashamed of myself. There was a humility I've tried to find since. But goodness wears off. And it just gets easier to be a contrary bollocks.

Down in the garage. Spinning small jobs out all day. Taking hours to fix a puncture. Stops you thinking about what might have been and what you should have done. It's like looking away. Like I did at that reception. You should only catch some-one's eye for the right reason. And I'll tell you – there's not one morning I don't wake up with her name in the room. (*Pause.*)

And I do be at this fella. Don't I? (*Pause.*) Yep. (*Pause.*) I may be on my way now.

BRENDAN. Will you be okay in that wind?

JACK. Jaysus, I should be used to that road by now, says you, ha?

BRENDAN. I'll get you the torch.

JACK. Am I a moaner?

BRENDAN (*going*). There's well fucking worse, I'll tell you. (*Exits.*)

JACK. Well. That wasn't a ghostly story. Anyway. At least, ha?

VALERIE. No.

JACK. We've had enough of them. (*Pause.*) We'll all be ghosts soon enough, says you, ha?

VALERIE. Mmm.

JACK. We'll all be sitting here. Sipping whiskey all night with Maura Nealon. (*Pause.*) Yeah. (*Short pause.*) This has been a strange little evening for me.

VALERIE (*a little laugh*). For me as well.

JACK. Fuck. We could do worse. It was lovely to meet you.

VALERIE. You too.

JACK. I didn't mean to go on there.

VALERIE. No, please . . .

JACK. Something about your company. Inspiring, ha? And this of course. (*Glass.*)

They smile.

I wonder if being out here in the country is the best place for you to . . . you know . . .

VALERIE. Why?

JACK. Ah. Girl like you. Hiding yourself away. Listening to old headers like us talking about the fairies. Having all your worst fears confirmed for you. Tuh. Ghosts and angels and all this?

Fuck them. I won't have it. Because I won't see someone like you being upset by it. You've enough to . . . deal with, for fuck's sake. I am very, sorry, love, about what happened.

VALERIE. Thanks.

BRENDAN *comes in turning the torch on and off.*

BRENDAN. The batteries are a bit weak. Come on, I'll drop you.

JACK. Are you sure?

BRENDAN. Sure, I'm giving Valerie a lift.

VALERIE. Come with us.

JACK. Okay, then. Grand.

BRENDAN *is clearing glasses, going in behind the bar, tidying up.*

VALERIE. Do you want a hand, Brendan?

BRENDAN. Oh no! Stay where you are, I'll be finished in a sec.

JACK *takes his anorak, joking.*

JACK. Is this yours, Valerie?

VALERIE. Yeah right.

JACK *takes her jacket and holds it for her to put on.*

JACK. Come on.

VALERIE. Oh now. Very nice.

JACK. These are the touches, ha, Brendan?

BRENDAN. That's them.

JACK. Now.

VALERIE. Thanks.

JACK. Mmm. Have a last fag I think.

Taking cigarette packet.

Anyone else?

VALERIE. No, I won't thanks.

BRENDAN. No, I'm grand thanks, Jack.

JACK. Up early in the morning. Over to Conor Boland. He's over the other side of Carrick there. Has about fifteen fucking kids. Dirty bollocks.

BRENDAN *and* VALERIE *laugh.*

JACK. And you should see her. Built like a fucking tractor. The head on her.

BRENDAN. You're a terrible man.

JACK. I've had my moments.

BRENDAN *looks at* VALERIE *and shakes his head.*

VALERIE. Will you be in here again soon?

JACK. Ah I'm always in and out. Got to keep the place afloat at least, you know?

BRENDAN (*working*). Don't mind him now, Valerie. Him and the Jimmy fella'll be fierce scarce around here the next few weeks.

VALERIE. Why?

BRENDAN (*stops work and lights a cigarette*). All the Germans'll be coming and they love it in here.

VALERIE (*to* JACK). You don't like that?

JACK *makes a face.*

BRENDAN. He thinks they're too noisy.

JACK. See, you don't know what they do be saying or anything.

BRENDAN. Him and Jimmy be sitting there at the bar with big sour pusses on them. Giving out like a couple of old grannies.

JACK. Ah we're not that bad.

BRENDAN. You're like a pair of bloody auld ones, you should see them.

VALERIE. Where do you go instead?

JACK. Ah, place down in Carrick, the Pot.

BRENDAN (*derision*). 'The Pot', There does be just as many of them down there don't be codding yourself.

JACK. Ah no, it doesn't seem as bad down there, now.

VALERIE. That's because this is your place.

JACK. Now. You've hit it on the head. You see, Brendan, Valerie's defending us. It's out of respect for this place.

BRENDAN. It is in my fucking barney respect! The two of yous leaving me standing behind that bar with my arms folded, picking my hole and not knowing what the hell is going on. And them playing all old sixties songs on their guitars. And they don't even know the words.

And nothing for me to do except pull a few pints and watch the shadow from the Knock moving along the floor, with the sun going down. I'm like some fucking mentler, I do be watching it! Watching it creeping up on the Germans. And they don't even notice it. I must be cracking up if that's my entertainment of an evening.

JACK. Ah don't be moaning. I'll tell you what. If Valerie's willing to come in and brave the Germans, then I'm sure me and Jim'll come in and keep yous company, hows that now?

BRENDAN. Oh you'll *grace* us with your ugly mushes, will you?

JACK. Don't push it, boy. Ah sure, Jaysus, what am I talking about?

Sure you'll have Finbar in here sniffing around Valerie every night anyway.

VALERIE. Ah now stop.

They laugh a little.

JACK. He'll be like a fly on a big pile of shite, so he will. Jesus. That came out all wrong, didn't it?

BRENDAN. No Jack. That was perfect. As usual.

JACK. Couldn't have come out worse. Sorry about that.

VALERIE. Would you relax?

BRENDAN *is putting his jacket on.*

JACK. Sorry. Will you anyway?

VALERIE. What? Come in . . . with the . . . Germans?

JACK. Yeah.

VALERIE. Doesn't bother me.

JACK. Ah, I think that's the right attitude. You should stay with the company and the bright lights.

BRENDAN (*looking around*). Do you see my keys?

VALERIE *and* JACK *look around a little bit.*

VALERIE. Sure I might even learn some German.

JACK. Ah, I don't know. They're eh . . . Are they from Germany, 'Brendan?

BRENDAN. What?

JACK. The Germans. (*To* VALERIE.) We call them the Germans.

VALERIE *picks keys off the mantelpiece.*

VALERIE. Is this them?

BRENDAN. Yeah, thanks. Are we right?

They are moving towards the door.

JACK. Where are they from. Is it Denmark, or Norway? (*To* VALERIE.) It's somewhere like that.

JACK *goes out, followed by* VALERIE.

BRENDAN. Ah I don't know where the fuck they're from.

BRENDAN *turns off the light and leaves.*

Slow fade.